Diana Poulton: A Tutor for the Renaissance Lute

DIANA POULTON

A Tutor for the Renaissance Lute

for the complete beginner
to the advanced student

ED 12324

Mainz · London · Berlin · Madrid · New York · Paris · Prague · Tokyo · Toronto

First published in 1991
by Schott Music Ltd, London
48 Great Marlborough Street
London W1F 7BB

© 1991 Schott Music Ltd, London

British Library Cataloguing in Publication Data
Poulton, Diana
   A tutor for the Renaissance lute: for the complete
   beginner to the advanced student.
   1. Lute—Performance
   I. Title
   787'.67'0714   ML 1013

ISMN 979-0-2201-1526-4
ED 12324

Designed by Olivia Kilmartin

Music setting by Andrew Jones

Typeset in 11 on 13 point Plantin
by York House Typographic Ltd

All rights reserved.
Printed in Germany.

No part of this publication
may be reproduced, stored in
a retrieval system, or transmitted
in any form or by any means, electronic,
mechanical, photocopying, recording or otherwise,
without the prior written permission of the publishers.

Contents

Introduction .... *page* 1
    The instrument 1
    Stringing 2
    Tuning 2
    Some practical advice on tuning 3
    Tablature 4
    Holding the Lute 6

The Lessons
    1: The right hand 7
    2: The left hand 9
    3 11
    4 17
    5 19
    6 24
    7: The diapasons 25
    8 32
    9 35
    10 39
    11: Italian tablature 40
    12: The hexachord 50
    13: Spanish music and the vihuela 51
    14: More about Spanish music 61
          Questions 67
    15: Scales 68
    16: The use of graces in Renaissance lute music 71
    17: The performing of graces 77
    18 78
    19: Graces in English sources 83
    20: Intabulations of polyphonic vocal music 95
    21: The interpretation of signs in the French *air de cour* 103
    22: The 'half' *barré* 106
    23: German tablature 107
    24: *Cifra nueva* 125
    25: The ten-course lute 130
    26 134

List of Sources and Modern Editions 140

Acknowledgements

The publishers would like to thank the following libraries for permission to reproduce material from their collections:

The British Library, London
pp. 27, 51, 83, 88-89, 89-91, 104-105 and 106

Staatsbibliothek Preußischer Kulturbesitz, Berlin
pp. 36, 95 and 98

Bibliothèque du Conservatoire, Bibliothèque Nationale, Paris
pp. 37-39

Österreichische Nationalbibliothek, Vienna
pp. 48-49, 108-113, 114-115, 116-117, 117-119 and 120

Folger Shakespeare Library, Washington, D.C.
pp. 86-87

Národní Knihovna, Prague
p. 122

Musikbibliothek der Stadt Leipzig, Leipzig
p. 123

Biblioteca Nacional, Madrid
pp. 125 and 126-127

The lute roses, set as illustrative devices on pp. 6, 85, 121, 124 and 127, are taken from instruments made by Stephen Barber and Sandi Harris, London, and are reproduced here by kind permission.

Author's Note

My thanks are due to Tim Crawford for his invaluable help in correcting the proofs.

Introduction

There is no doubt that for anyone who has the opportunity to study with a good teacher much time can be saved and the initial difficulties straightened out more easily. There are still, however, many places where no teacher is available and, in this *Tutor for the Renaissance Lute*, I have attempted to set out a series of lessons which should save the beginner from the time-wasting and disheartening work of trying to find a way to proficiency by trial and error. Without help or guidance in the early stages it is all too easy to fall into habits which may, eventually, hold up further progress.

As with all instruments and music in general, the lute and its music underwent a process of change and development, a process which eventually led to a complete distinction of two styles now generally known as Renaissance and Baroque. However, since these changes came about at different times in different countries, it is impossible to set a hard-and-fast date to which the two terms can be applied.

There was, of course, an intermediate period during which both the earlier instrument and its music predominated, but changes, such as the modification of technique, the addition of more bass courses and some experimental alterations in the basic tuning, began to show themselves. Eventually there emerged an instrument with differences in both shape and sound, music which retained hardly any characteristics of the earlier style and a technique which involved a radical change in the position of the right hand.

The lessons in this book will deal with the lute and its technique from the earliest sources of information up to the end of the time when the type of instrument and its music can, with any justification, be described as belonging to the Renaissance.

The technique which will be taught is based on many years of study of the instructions contained in a number of books, both printed and in manuscript, having their origin in many different countries during the sixteenth and seventeenth centuries. But one of the great difficulties of reconstructing a 'method' for the Renaissance lute is the fact that, during the period of its greatest flowering, no really complete book of instruction was ever produced. Some writers will provide excellent advice on certain points but on others of equal importance nothing is said and a search has to be made to see whether the information can be found elsewhere. Whether it is true or not, a reason for this shortcoming, often given at the time, was that teachers were unwilling to disclose fully the secrets of their own mastery of the instrument. Another reason may have been that some of the basic facts were so well known that it was considered unnecessary to mention them. Such instructions as do exist are generally placed at the beginning of the book, but except in the case of some of the early German masters such as Hans Newsidler and Hans Gerle and, to a certain extent the Spaniard, Luys Milan, there is hardly any pedagogic system and no attempt is made to lead the beginner gently from the easiest pieces to those of more technical difficulty.*

The instrument

If you have not already bought a lute it is most desirable that you should first seek expert advice. You can waste both time and money by buying an instrument which is not well adjusted in all details or which is unsuitable for your purpose.

---

*Thomas Mace, in his *Musick's Monument* (1676; facsimile reprint, C.N.R.S., 1966), gives more detailed and precise instructions than any other writer on the lute. Unfortunately, by his time, the tuning, the fashion in music and the style of play had all changed so radically that much of what he says is inapplicable to the earlier period. *The Burwell Lute Tutor* (facsimile reprint, Boethius Press, 1974), being almost contemporary with Mace, has the same drawback.

In trying to trace the development of the lute it becomes clear that changes of fashion occur in different countries at different times, but even so, these changes are not necessarily consistent since preferences between one player and another can also be clearly seen. For example, evidence suggests that at the beginning of the period with which we are now dealing the lute had six courses, each course consisting of two strings, except in the case of the top course which could be either single or double. Hans Newsidler, the great teacher from Nuremberg, in a book printed in 1536, shows a diagram of a six-course lute with a single top string. In a diagram of an Italian lute in an instruction sheet by Michele Carrara, printed in Rome in 1585, all the courses are double. In Adrian Le Roy's book, which appeared in an English translation under the title *A Briefe and easye instru[c]tion* in 1568, a woodcut shows a lute of six courses with a single top string. Yet Thomas Robinson, in 1603, makes it clear that his lute was strung with double courses throughout and John Dowland, in 'Other Necessary Observations belonging to the Lute' in *Varietie of Lute-Lessons* (1610), implies that his lute also had a double top course.

As early as 1511 a seventh course was mentioned but no music from that date includes its use. By 1585 eight courses are shown on the previously mentioned instruction sheet by Michele Carrara. These extra courses were known as diapasons. For some years to come, however, the greater part of the lute repertoire was still being written for a six-course instrument. By the beginning of the seventeenth century nine courses were in use and a tenth course was added soon after. This was the limit of the true Renaissance instrument.

Stringing

Until the introduction of metal-wound overspun strings for the lower courses in the 1660s (their invention is first mentioned by John Playford in 1664), the lute was strung throughout with gut. Although there is no doubt that the sound of gut is much sweeter than that of nylon and that covered strings for the lower courses give a different sound, it is advisable for the beginner to start with nylon strings since, once the instrument has settled in tune, they are far less susceptible to changes of temperature and humidity than gut. Later, the choice remains open and there are some professional players today who find the extra tuning problems are compensated for by the sweetness and authenticity of the sound.

Tuning

The tuning of the six-course lute is made up of fourths with a third in the middle. Lutes of different sizes, to be tuned at different pitches, were in use during the Renaissance period and, of course, they are made today, but the tuning in most general use consists of the following notes reading from the sixth course upwards: G c f a d' and g'.

At the beginning of the period with which we are dealing the three lower courses were tuned in octaves. Towards the end of the sixteenth century, however, some players began to use unison stringing throughout and, by 1610, John Dowland, in *Varietie of Lute-Lessons*, comments that octave strings were considered to be 'irregular to the rules of Musicke'.

The tuning of the diapasons varies greatly. It can be arranged in any of the following ways for a seven- to a ten-course lute:

7th course	F or D
7th and 8th	F and D
	F and E (or E flat)
	F and C
7th, 8th and 9th	F E (or E flat) and D
	F E (or E flat) and C
7th, 8th, 9th and 10th	F E (or E flat) D and C

Very rarely the 10th is lowered to B or B flat.

Introduction

In the case of the seven-course lute, if the seventh is strung to be tuned at D it will only be possible to raise it to F if gut strings are used, but the D tuning is probably the most useful since in many cases it is possible to obtain the F by stopping the third fret. This was often done. Nevertheless, as will be seen later, some pieces are written for the F tuning and in such a way that the desired effect is almost impossible to produce if the F does not come from the open string.

Directions for the tuning of the diapasons are seldom given in original sources so, where they do appear, before playing a piece it is necessary to examine the chords or notes under which they occur in order to determine to which note each one should be tuned.

Some practical advice on tuning

The following hints are intended only for the student who has had no previous experience of tuning a musical instrument.

It is not uncommon to find a beginner, wrestling with the early difficulties of tuning, with pegs in a condition which makes success impossible. If the pegs slip a reliable preparation can be bought from most musical instrument dealers, or powdered resin can be used. If they stick, a little French chalk can be used, but care must be taken not to use too much. Sometimes it will be found that when a peg is turned the string either does not move or it moves with a sudden jerk. This means it is not slipping properly over the fret-nut. This can be cured by loosening the string and rubbing the groove with a well-sharpened lead pencil.

There will be the same number of pegs in the peg-box as there are strings, and on these pegs the strings should be arranged in the following order: with the soundboard of the lute facing you, the pegs on the right-hand side will carry the strings highest in pitch. Assuming that you are using a single first course, this will be wound on the peg nearest the fret-nut; the first string of the second course on the second peg; the second string of the second course on the third peg. The rest should follow in exact order, away from you down the right-hand side and towards you up the left-hand side ending with the lowest course on the two pegs nearest the fret-nut. The exact order is essential. For tuning it is important to know by touch the exact point where each string is controlled. If the order of the stringing is altered it will greatly increase the difficulties.

In the actual winding of the string onto the peg, be sure that the winding ends on the side of the peg nearest the inner cheek of the peg-box so that the tension is pulling inwards. If the winding ends towards the thinner end of the peg the tension will press the peg outwards.

It will often be found in books in which polyphonic vocal music has been arranged for solo voice and lute that the soprano vocal line is given in the original key. If this were to be followed exactly, lutes at three, or even four pitches, would be required. That this was not the intention, however, is made clear by Franciscus Bossinensis in his *Libro Secondo*, printed in Venice in 1511. Here he gives an instruction before each vocal line as, for example, to tune the voice 'to the fifth fret of the canto', i.e., the highest course. In any case, it would probably have been necessary to give the singer (if it were not the lutenist himself) the starting note, since evidence suggests that during the sixteenth century pitch for instruments of the lute family was far from standardized. Even as relatively late as the early years of the seventeenth century, lack of a standard pitch was still common. For example, Thomas Robinson, in *The Schoole of Musicke* (printed in 1603), gives the instruction 'first set up the Treble, so high as you dare venture for breaking, setting them both in one tune or sound called an unison'.

Today it is the usual practice to have a lute for solo playing tuned to a nominal G, although some performers prefer to tune to F sharp or F according to the length of the strings and whether or not gut is used. Whichever note is chosen for the highest string the most convenient way for the beginner to tune is to take each note from a well-tuned keyboard, if one is available. If not, a tuning fork should be bought for the note of the third course, relative to the note chosen for the top string. For a top string at G it will be A440; for F sharp it will be G sharp, at F it will be G.

Start with one string of the third course. The tuning fork will sound an octave above the note to which it must be tuned, but your ear will soon become accustomed to this. There are several good reasons for starting with this string. Now bring the next string of the course into tune with it. Then you should proceed upwards with the second course and then with the first. Should you, to begin with, find difficulty in hearing the intervals, you can help yourself by using the gut frets which are set at semitone intervals on the neck of the lute. With a finger of the left hand stop the course you have just tuned on the fifth fret. When you play this string with a finger of the right hand it will give you the note to which the second course should be tuned. First tune one of the strings and then bring the other into tune with it. Similarly, the fifth fret of the second course will give you the note to which the top course must be tuned. Stop the third course on the third fret and bring the fifth course into tune with it an octave lower. Next, stop the fifth course on the fifth fret—and this will give you the note for the fourth course. The note to which the sixth course has to be tuned can be found (an octave higher) on the second fret of the fourth course. This should then be exactly two octaves below your first course. If your lute has octave stringing on the three lower courses, follow these instructions for the lower string of the course and then bring the higher octave into tune.

Once you have tuned your lute, check it regularly with a keyboard or tuning fork to ensure that the pitch is maintained exactly.

However, in music written for a G to g' lute, whatever pitch is chosen, the notes have to be thought of as G c f a d' g', otherwise in reading from staff notation, unless another pitch is actually stated, the notes will come on the wrong positions on the fingerboard and in transcribing from tablature the music will end up in the wrong key. From now onwards whenever notes of the scale are mentioned they will be referred to as they would occur in the G tuning, unless some other pitch is indicated in the original source.

Tablature

Music for the lute is written in a form of notation called tablature. Tablature for other instruments exists, but this particular form came into use in answer to the special needs of the lute and other stringed instruments of the same kind. For this purpose it has many advantages in representing the composer's intention. It is also much easier to read onto the lute than staff notation.

There are several different forms of lute tablature all of which will be explained in due course. English lutenists normally used the system known as French tablature, and this will be explained first.

Unlike staff notation, tablature deals only with the positions of the fingers and not with musical sounds. The six-line stave represents the six main courses of the lute. The letters disposed on or between the lines denote the positions in which the fingers are to be placed on the courses and the frets. In French tablature the letters are generally written above the line and not on it, although this is not invariably so. The top line of the stave represents the first course—that is the course highest in pitch. The second line represents the second course, the third line the third course, and so on down to the lowest line which represents the sixth course. All the open courses are represented by the letter *a*. All courses when stopped on the first fret are represented by the letter *b*; on the second fret by *c*; on the third fret by *d*; on the fourth by *e*; on the fifth by *f*, and thus the alphabet is followed up to *g*, *h* and *i*. No *j* is used so *i* is followed by *k* and as many other letters as are needed. Some lutes have extra frets made of wood and glued to the soundboard, but others may have none, in which case the high notes have to be found with the fingers alone. By these means a precise plan is given of where the fingers of the left hand are to be placed, and which courses are to be played with the right hand. On the following page is a diagram, going up to fret *f*, which will make this clear.

The diapasons are indicated in a number of different ways:

7th course	*a*	*ā*	*a*	
8th course	/*a*	/*ā*	/*a*	*a*/
9th course	//*a*	//*ā*	*a*	*a*//
10th course	///*a*	///*ā*	///*a*	*a*///

Course	Open	1st fret	2nd fret	3rd fret	4th fret	5th fret
1	a	b	c	d	e	f
2	a	b	c	d	e	f
3	a	b	c	d	e	f
4	a	b	c	d	e	f
5	a	b	c	d	e	f
6	a	b	c	e	d	f

Jean-Baptiste Besard's use of signs in the *Thesaurus Harmonicus* (1603) can be rather confusing. He uses ᴀ for the seventh course and a capital A for the eighth course. When he wants the notes D, E and F he uses the capital letters ACD, or for D, E and F sharp he uses ACE. For the note C he uses a Gothic type 𝔄.

The duration of the note or chord is indicated by signs placed over the stave. In sixteenth- and seventeenth-century books of instruction the signs are given the following values:

| or ↑ = o   Semibreve

⌐ = 𝅗𝅥   Minim

⌐ (with tail) = 𝅘𝅥   Crotchet

⌐ (with two tails) = 𝅘𝅥𝅮   Quaver

⌐ (with three tails) = 𝅘𝅥𝅯   Semiquaver

Every further tail added to the stem divides the note by half. No time-mark longer than | (a semibreve), is used. The tails which are added to the stem have no other significance at all beyond their relation to this basic time value. They give no indication of speed. Thus four ⌐ in a bar can represent the very moderate 4/4 of a pavan, and six of them in a bar can represent the very rapid 6/8 of a jig. In a great quantity of lute music, particularly in the manuscripts, no time signature is given at the beginning of a piece. Careful consideration therefore has to be given to the form and character of the piece before its speed can be determined.

A dot following one of the time-marks has precisely the same significance as in staff notation, i.e., it prolongs the note by half its duration.

The way in which the above signs were actually written varies considerably. In printed tablature it is more usual to find the 'signal' type of sign, as in the examples given above. This type holds good for the note over which it is placed and all those that follow until a new sign is given.

Thus ⌐   ⌐ indicates four minims followed by four crotchets.
     a a a a a a a a

In manuscripts, however, a kind of gridiron is often used. In this system four quavers followed by four semiquavers would be expressed like this:
     a a a a   a a a a

Where the value of a single note is to be expressed the 'signal' type is used.

In many modern transcriptions the value of these signs is halved.

Holding the lute

First it is important to find a chair that suits your height. If the chair is too high it will greatly increase your initial difficulties.

From a study of pictures through the centuries it can be seen that lutes were held in a number of different positions. Some players are shown standing, others sitting with both feet firmly planted on the ground; some use a low footstool for the left foot, others sit with one leg crossed over the other. In many pictures the lute is shown resting on, or supported by, a table and this support is recommended in several of the books of instruction. From these various positions the student should choose the one in which he or she feels most comfortable and relaxed.

The back of the lute rests against the diaphragm of the player and the lower edge rests on the thigh. The right forearm, as it comes over the upper edge of the lute for the hand to touch the courses, exerts a light pressure so that the weight of the instrument is taken by neither hand. It is largely a matter of finding exactly how to balance the lute so that it rests in position even when neither hand is touching it.

It is important that it should be held so that the soundboard is facing slightly upwards and not in a position which projects the sound towards the floor.

The Lessons

Lesson 1:
The right hand

The finger nails must be short and must not touch the courses in playing. Except for one Italian teacher, Alessandro Piccinini, in 1623, this point is constantly emphasized, and even he only advocates that the nail should be gently rounded to coincide with the tip of the finger. Thomas Mace, in 1676, suggests they may be used in consort playing. The long nails of the present-day guitar player will produce an entirely unauthentic sound.

To bring the hand into the correct position the forearm should touch the upper edge of the lute just about level with the bridge. The hand is held obliquely across the strings continuing the line of the arm and, in the technique now being described, not at a right angle across the strings. The little finger is laid on the soundboard. This is a point of great importance and is mentioned in every book of instruction in which the right-hand technique is described. It will lie with the side, and not the tip, touching the soundboard. Although, with this type of technique, the thumb and first finger may touch the courses across the lower end of the rose, it is not usual for the hand to be held directly over the rose as in modern guitar playing.

The movement of the hand up and down the strings in order to change the kind of tone produced is only mentioned by one writer, Piccinini, who appears to have been somewhat eccentric in his time. Other writers, in describing how the little finger is laid on the soundboard use such phrases as 'this is its constant position' or 'as if [it] were glued unto it'.

Single notes are played with the thumb and first finger alternately, the thumb always taking the accented note. Later this technique was modified, but it is essential to master this type of fingering before proceeding further. All through this book, where the right-hand fingering is indicated, the conventional signs of a small stroke for the thumb and a dot placed under the note for the first finger, will be used.

Firstly, it is essential to acquire command of the correct movement of the thumb. With the hand in the position already described and with the thumb held low and almost parallel with the sixth course, it should move forward and downward as if it were going to touch the second finger; the course will then be touched with the side of the thumb and not with the tip. This movement should bring the thumb to rest on the course immediately next to it: that is, if the thumb is moving from the sixth course it should come to rest on the fifth. This ensures that both strings of the course are sounded.

Practise this movement across the strings as follows:

When this has been mastered practise the movement in reverse:

Now work backwards and forwards without looking at your hand until you begin to feel the movement with some degree of certainty. Later, more information will be given about this special movement of the thumb and why it is important.

Next the movement of the first finger must be mastered. The finger should be slightly curved and the tip must be laid on the course so that both strings are touched. The movement of the finger is not carried through to touch the next course.

Practise this movement downwards and upwards:

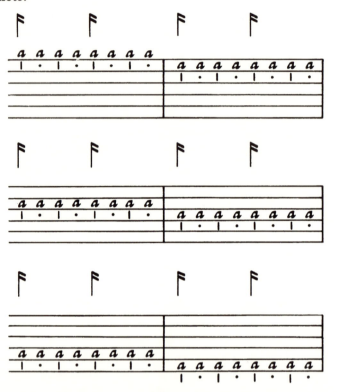

Passages of single notes are played with the thumb and the first finger used alternately but in this case the movement of the thumb has to be slightly modified and, while still exerting the downwards pressure, it must be lifted just before it touches the next course. The thumb always takes the accented note.

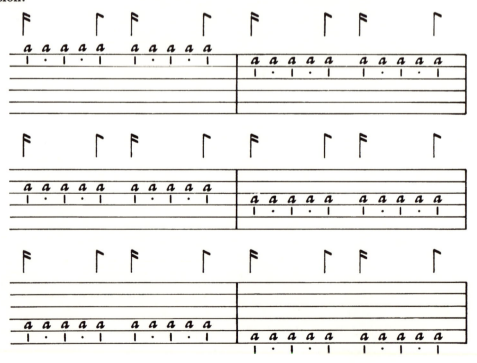

When one accented note is followed by another accented note the thumb is used twice in succession:

Here is a more complicated rhythmic pattern in which the same type of fingering must be used:

Lesson 2:
The left hand

Allow the left arm to fall into a natural, relaxed position at your side, then lift your hand and place it on the neck of the lute with the thumb on the back of the neck between the first and the second frets; the knuckles should be raised so that the hand is curved and the tips of the fingers fall on the courses. The elbow should be raised slightly from your side so that the forearm and the fingers are parallel with the frets. The thumb and the first finger should be in such a position that they would meet if the neck of the lute were not there. This is the basic position of the left hand. It is of great importance that no weight is taken by this hand and that the thumb rests only lightly on the back of the neck so that it may not in any way impede the movement of the rest of the hand.

In the next exercise the thumb should be placed between the joint of the neck and the peg-box and the first fret. Place the first finger just behind fret b. (The fingers should never be placed actually on the frets; it will deaden the sound.) With the right hand play ♭ ♩ with the thumb and first finger. When the left-hand finger moves across towards the fourth, fifth and sixth courses the wrist should rise a little and the thumb should move slightly towards the palm of the hand. In this way the curved position can be maintained and the tip of the finger will fall onto the lower courses. Without this movement the finger will have to be stretched forward and it will only be possible to lay the front of the finger on the courses:

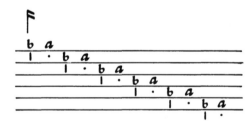

Now reverse the movement, but in moving backwards care should be taken not to allow the left hand to fall into a position where the base of the first finger touches the side of the fingerboard, or the neck to sink down between the thumb and base of the first finger. There must always be a clear space under the fingers at this point.

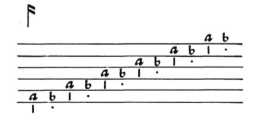

Next, put the thumb between the first and second fret on the back of the neck and use the second finger for the note c:

With the thumb in the same place, the first and second fingers will now be used. In this kind of movement when, as in this case, *b* is stopped with the first finger and *c* with the second, after the *b* has been played the first finger should not be lifted until the *c* has been played. Both are then lifted simultaneously.

In using these two fingers in the reverse order both should be placed on the course before the first note is struck. When the *c* has been played the second finger is lifted; *b* is then played, the first finger is then lifted and both are placed simultaneously on the next course.

It is important to acquire the ability to move the fingers in these two ways since both contribute greatly to the continuity and smoothness of sound.

Another important point, which should be studied right from the first, is to keep the fingers as close as possible to the courses, only just lifting them clear. If they fly upwards with uncontrolled movements it will eventually become harder to play really rapid passages since the further the fingers travel away from the strings, the longer it takes for them to return. Also, untidy fingers are disturbing to an audience.

Now add the third finger to the two that have been used already. The small numbers under the sixth line indicate which finger to use. Where two stopped notes occur on the same string, remember the directions in the last two exercises, and follow the right-hand fingering carefully.

In the next exercise, when the fourth finger stops the letter *f* on the first course, it will be necessary to place the thumb between the second and the third fret. When the *d* and *c* are stopped on the second course with the second and first finger the thumb should be allowed to come back into position between the first and second fret. Again it will be necessary to allow it to follow the movement of the hand when the final notes of the scale are played. Place the fourth, third and first fingers in position before the first note is struck.

Lesson 2,3

Lesson 3

It is now time to return to the right hand and to combine the use of the thumb with the first and second fingers in a treble and bass line. The second finger is marked with two dots. Where two notes come together the higher of the pair must be played with the second finger. At first take this exercise slowly with the movement of the thumb being as described in the first exercise. Let it come to rest on the fifth course, then lift it and play the next note in the treble line.

In the piece which follows* the right and the left hand must now work together. Where two notes occur they must be struck simultaneously with the second finger and thumb of the right hand. In the left hand the letter c should be taken with the first finger and the letter d with the second. Follow the right-hand fingering carefully.

No. 1

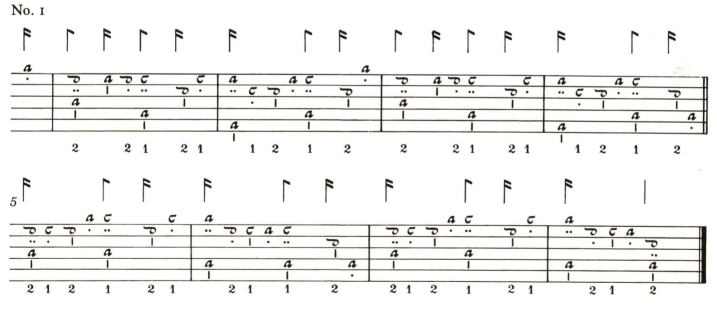

Ein Niderlendisch tentzlein

The first and second fingers of the left hand will be used in the same way in the following piece, except in bar 6 where the second finger must be used for c on the third course. For the present the signs ♯ and + in bars 4 and 8 should be ignored; they indicate graces and will be explained later.

*A list of sources is provided at the end of this book and the origin of each piece can be found under its appropriate number.

No. 2

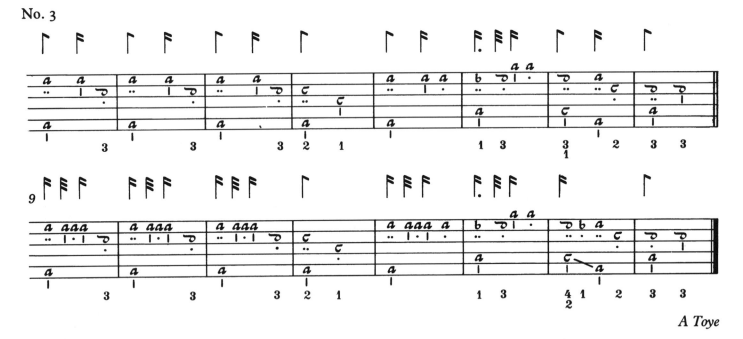

Pegaramsey

All fingering is marked in the next piece and should be followed carefully with both hands. In bars 7 and 15 two notes must be stopped with the left hand. In bar 15, *c* on the fifth course must be held until it is time to play *a* on the sixth course. The conventional mark for this is a line connecting the two notes.

No. 3

A Toye

Here is another piece in two parts—treble and bass. If this were transcribed into staff notation the rhythm would be shown as 6/8. From now on, unless otherwise marked, it should be assumed that all bass notes are played with the thumb.

No. 4

Lesson 3

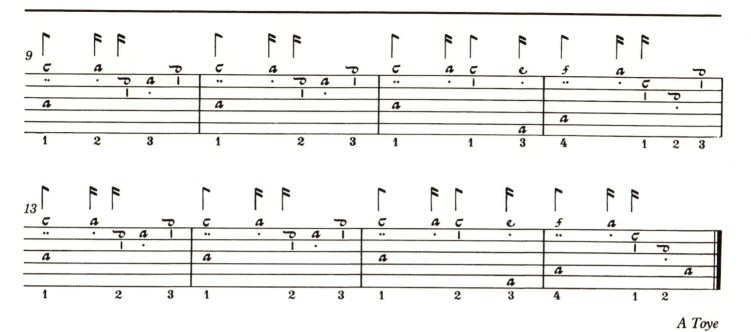

A Toye

Continuing with simple pieces in two parts, two fingers of the left hand will now need to be used more frequently. As you will see, the first finger for fret *c* and the second for fret *d* are generally used, but in bars 7, 8 and 9, and other similar passages, it is better to take the second and third fingers in bar 7, as the first and second will be needed in bar 9. In bar 10 the first finger must be placed on *c* on the fifth course and held in position through the next two bars. The second finger will be needed for *c* on fret 2 on the second course in bar 12.

Where there is insufficient room to place the right-hand fingering marks under the letters they are placed beside them.

No. 5

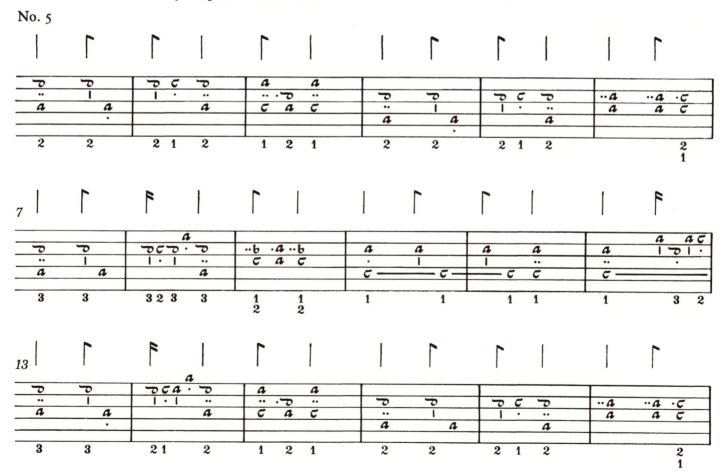

Ein guter Hofftanz

From now on attention must be paid to holding the bass notes whether they are marked or not.

In sixteenth-century Germany the 'Hofftanz' was often followed by the 'hupff auff' which consisted of the same musical material arranged in triple time.

No. 6

Lesson 3

Der hupff auff zum Hofftanz

In all of the following works the usual method of indicating the right-hand fingering will be used, that is: dots will be placed under those notes which are struck with the first or second finger but the thumb will not be indicated unless it is used in some unusual circumstance. Futhermore, in order to avoid circumlocution, the courses will be referred to, from the top line of the stave to the bottom, as 1 to 6. Thus the first two notes in the next piece would be referred to as *b* on 3 and *d* on 6.

Where a time-mark occurs with no chord or note under it, it has here the same meaning as a rest.

When the third finger of the left hand is used to stop the sixth course, as in bars 1 and 2 of the next piece, it is important that the wrist should be raised slightly so that the finger can fall on the course as nearly as possible in the same position in which it falls on the other courses. If the thumb is held lightly enough it will move slightly under the hand towards the wrist thus allowing the finger to stop the course with the tip. The finger must be kept very still or it will kill the sound before its due time.

No. 7

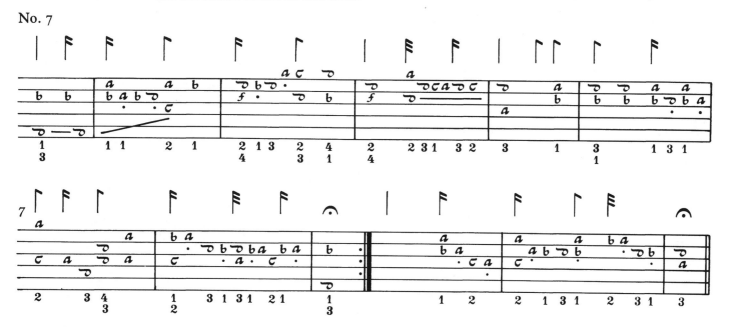

Nach Willen Dein

It is useful, at this point, to turn the first two bars into the following exercise:

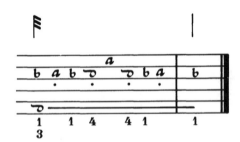

Watch the third finger to see that it remains quite still and that the sound of *d* on 6 is maintained until the final *b* on 3 has been played.

When this has been mastered try this slightly more difficult one:

Lesson 4

In three-note chords the right-hand fingering, reading from the lowest note upwards, is thumb, first finger, second finger.

Towards the end of the sixteenth century the strict observance of the alternating use of the thumb and first finger began to be modified in favour of using the first and second finger in passages where a number of bass notes accompany the treble line. For rapid passages of single notes, however, the thumb-and-first-finger technique is still advocated as making greater speed possible. In the following piece, written out in the early years of the seventeenth century, the first-and-second-finger technique is clearly marked in some passages. Here it is marked throughout in order that the student may begin to learn this alternative method. Again, for the time being, ignore the sign ♯.

No. 8

Willsons Wilde

Lesson 4

In the following piece it will be more convenient to keep the thumb on the lower courses and use the first and second fingers on the melody line.

No. 9

Calleno

Both techniques could be combined in the next piece. Observe the held notes in the bass carefully. Practise of the little exercises following No. 7 should have helped to make it possible to hold the *d* on 4 and the *d* on 5 each time they occur.

No. 10

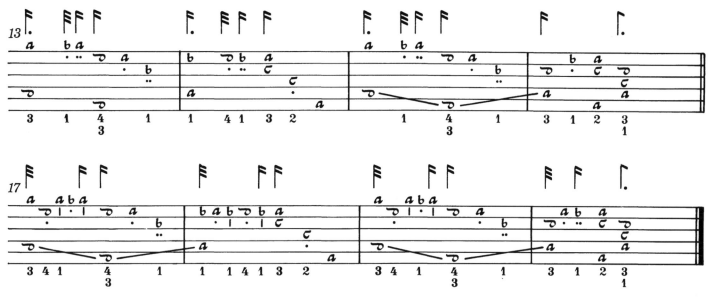

Packington's Pound

Lesson 5

In this lesson the student will begin to study the playing of chords of four or more notes.

When the fingers of the left hand are placed on the courses to stop the notes of the chord, the top joint of each finger should be as nearly as possible at a right angle to the fingerboard, so that the course is stopped with the tip of the finger only. When changing from one chord to another do not lift the hand from the first chord and then say 'What do I do now?', but before you play the first one, look at the second to see whether there is a note in common. If there is, then plan your fingering so that the same finger is used on that note in both chords. For example, take the following two chords. Put the left-hand fingers on as marked in the first chord:

Do not, for the moment, use the right hand, but practise the change to the next chord. Leave the second finger on *d* on the third course, move the first finger back to *c* on the first course and put the third down on the *d* on the second course. Change back to the first chord and repeat the movement several times without moving the second finger from its place on fret *d* on the third course. In this way contact with the courses will not be entirely abandoned. When this method of chord changing is mastered it helps enormously in finding the way about the fingerboard without looking and it plays an important part in maintaining continuity of sound.

Now with the right hand play the bass note with the thumb, the next note to it with the first finger, the next with the second and the top note of the chord with the third finger. In the case of the first chord the thumb should come forward to rest on the fourth course. In the second chord, while still exerting the downward pressure, it must stop just short of touching the next course. Practise changing the two chords, backwards and forwards, keeping the second finger in place all the time. Now take the next change:

With the fingers in place on the second of the two chords that have already been played, draw the second finger back from *d* on the third course to *c*, without lifting it; bring the first finger across from *c* on the first course to *c* on the fourth course, at the same time lifting the third finger from *d* on the second course.

The second of the next two chords requires a seventh course tuned to F. If you do not have this course on your lute, and when this change (both here and in the following piece) is treated purely as an exercise, this note may be omitted. To make this change, keep the third finger in place, put the fourth down on *d* on the second course and lift the first finger from *c* on the fourth course. If you have the seventh course, then with your right thumb, practise, without looking, the move backwards from the fifth to the seventh course:

Finally, before you lift the third and fourth fingers from the two *d*s, have the first and second fingers ready to place on the two *c*s. The thumb of the right hand should have come to rest on the sixth course, where it will be ready to play that note:

You now have fingering for all the chord changes in the following piece.

No. 11

The Buffens

Lesson 5

In the instructions of Hans Gerle (publications between 1532 and 1552) and Hans Newsidler (publications between 1536 and 1549) both of Nuremberg, it is said that some chords are played across the strings with the thumb but no special signs are given. In the publications from the Venetian printing firm of Petrucci (1507 to 1511) it is said that 'when more than one note has to be played, there being no dot present, it is necessary to play all downwards'. This somewhat ambiguous instruction is generally taken to mean that chords with notes on adjacent strings are to be played with the thumb. Later books show that the following method of playing such chords was used in France, England and Germany:

To play six-note chords:
    Strike the 6th and 5th courses downwards with the thumb;
    Strike the 3rd and 4th courses upwards with the first finger;
    Strike the 2nd course upwards with the second finger;
    Strike the 1st course upwards with the third finger.

To play five-note chords:
    Strike the 6th and 5th courses, or the 5th and 4th courses downwards with the thumb;
    Strike the other three courses upwards with the first, second and third fingers.

If, however, the bass note of the chord is separated from the other four notes as, for example, in the following chord:

then the seventh course is struck downwards with the thumb, the third and the fourth courses are struck upwards with the first finger and the second and first courses are played upwards with the second and first fingers.

In playing chords in this manner it is important that the hand should be completely relaxed so that the first finger can stroke gently across the top of the two courses, making sure that all four strings are touched. Played in this way a sound is produced which is characteristic of the lute and of no other instrument. With practice all the notes can be made to sound almost simultaneously if the chord is only of short duration or they can be somewhat spread if it occurs at the end of a section or as the final chord at the end of a composition. The following six-note chord should be practised in the way already described:

and then these five-note chords in the two ways according to whether or not the notes all lie on adjacent courses:

In the next piece chords of this type appear in the text.

No. 12

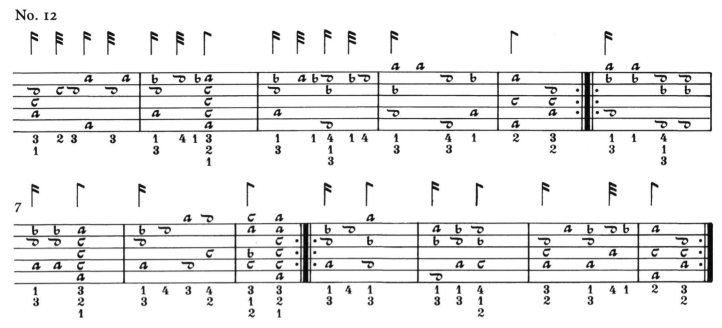

What if a day

Many chords and musical passages are found which can only be played by stopping more than one note with the first finger of the left hand. Take, for example, the following chord:

This can only be played by laying the first finger across the courses on fret *c* and then using the other fingers as marked. When the first finger is used in this way it is, nowadays, generally known as a *barré*.

In finding the right position in which to place the finger every student must experiment since the length and shape of the finger plays an important part in determining exactly how the courses can be covered so that each will sound clearly. Some players place the finger so that the sixth course is only just covered; others find it better to place the finger a little further over. Indeed, the position may vary a little according to which courses have to be covered. Much depends on finding how to avoid any of the courses that are to be stopped by this finger coinciding with the creases in the skin at the point directly under each joint. With practice it will be found that it is not necessary to exert a great deal of pressure from the thumb which will be in position under the first finger nor, as is sometimes seen, should the second finger be laid on top of the first in passages where this finger is free.

The use of *barré* is not always determined by a chord but, as can be seen in the following examples, by a decorative passage which follows it. Without a *barré* it would, in each case, be impossible to maintain the bass note for its full length.

Lesson 5

In practising these patterns care must be taken that the movement of the other fingers on the upper notes does not disturb the position of the first finger or the sound will be killed off before its due time.

In the next piece a *barré* should be used at the end of the fourth bar. Though it is possible to finger it without, it is much easier if a *barré* is used and it has the advantage of stopping the sound of the open sixth course (the note G) which should not continue under the chord of D major. *Barrés* should be used in the eighth and the ninth bar.

No. 13

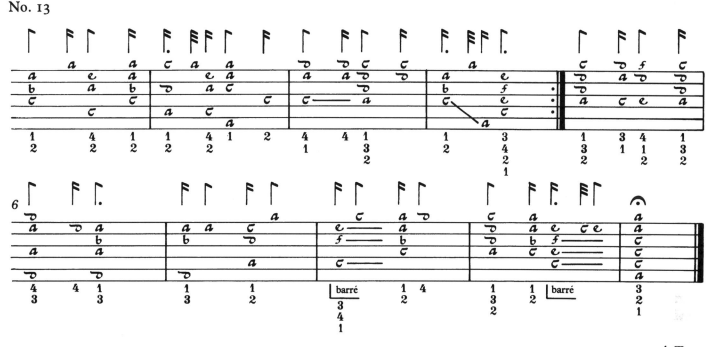

A Toye
[*Bara Faustus' Dream*]

Here are a few examples from among the many *barré* chords that will be met with sooner or later:

In order to gain individual control of each finger of the right hand in playing chords the following arpeggiated chords will be found useful. Each should be repeated several times as an exercise, care being taken that each finger produces an equal quality of sound. The left-hand fingering has been arranged in a way that would be convenient if the chords followed each other in a composition. When more than one note is stopped with the left hand all the necessary fingers should be placed on the strings before the first note is sounded. In number 8 care must be taken to ensure that the tip of the fourth finger falls on the letter *f* with the top joint as upright as possible.

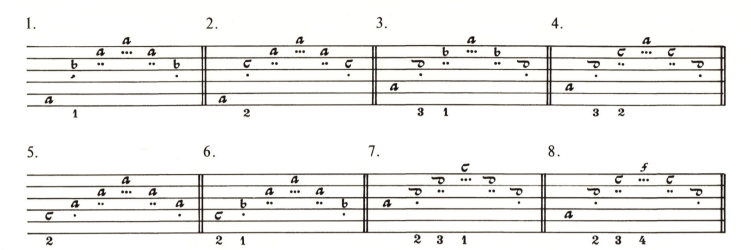

Arpeggiating the following *barré* chords in the same way will help greatly in showing whether any of the courses are not being properly covered by the first finger of the left hand.

Lesson 6

If you have already begun to associate the tablature signs with the actual music notes they represent, ignore this lesson; if not, you should now begin to do so. As you progress you will come to realize the many reasons which make this knowledge necessary. The best way to learn the positions of the notes is to begin gradually. Start by taking this first exercise and as you play each of the open strings repeat to yourself the appropriate note:

As each fret raises the sound by a semitone the notes across the second fret will be:

Those across the first fret will be sharps or flats according to the key:

Gradually, the notes that have been represented by tablature signs in the pieces already studied should be added to those now memorized. It will be found helpful if, from time to time, a piece is written out in staff notation. Here, for example, is No. 9, 'Calleno':

(Tablature note-values halved.)

When the 'basic' position of each note on the fingerboard has eventually been memorized, then what may, perhaps, be termed the 'misplaced' notes must also be learnt. These occur when a note cannot be played in its 'basic' position because the course on which it occurs is already occupied by another note, as, for example, in the following chord of D major:

These 'misplaced' positions are also used when the top note of a chord lies in a high position on the course and, to play the bass note in its normal position, would involve an impossible stretch for the left hand:

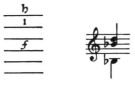

Lesson 7:
The diapasons

When the movement of the thumb was described in Lesson 1, it was said that more information would be given about the importance of this particular stroke. As soon as the use of the diapasons begins to be studied the need for the complete control of the thumb will become apparent.

In the next piece it will be assumed that the student has a lute with one diapason tuned at F, or that F is the first diapason if two or more are present. If there is no diapason at F it is better, for the present, to omit this piece and the one following, but whatever diapasons are brought into use, it will be found that the same kind of movement is necessary.

Before playing any of the notes which have to be stopped with the left hand and with the little finger of the right hand in place on the soundboard, practise the three bass notes with the thumb alone. Once the thumb is placed on the seventh course it is important not to look at the hand but to cultivate the sense of distance that the thumb has to travel. When the thumb has played the seventh course it will rest momentarily on the sixth; it will then jump over the sixth and come to rest on the fifth which it will then play coming to rest on the fourth which will finally be played. The touch on the string above the one that has been played is, of course, of the very shortest possible duration but the importance of it is that it forms a point of reference for the next movement. When a number of diapasons are used this point of reference is essential. If the thumb is allowed to fly upwards, away from the courses, the difficulty becomes almost impossible to overcome. When some degree of certainty has been achieved with the thumb, then the complete piece should be practised. In the first and second sections use the second and first fingers of the right hand on the melody line, but in the last section use the thumb and first finger on the single-note passages.

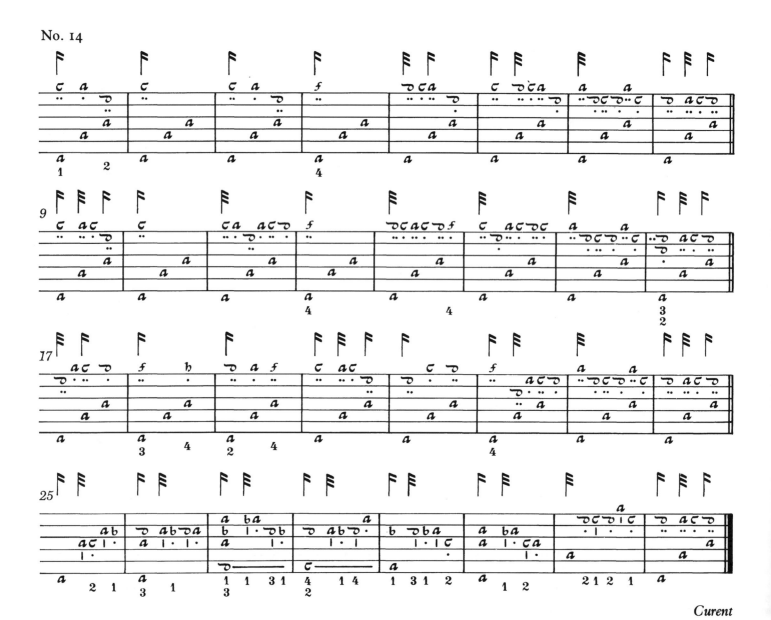

Curent

Lesson 7

In bar 2 of the next piece remember to keep the first finger in place on the letter *c* on 1 until *dfdc* have been played and in bar 3, before you play *d* on 1, put the first finger on *c* and keep it there until you have played *dcdc*. Use the same fingering on all similar patterns.

From time to time a piece will be reproduced in facsimile so that the student may become familiar with the appearance of some original sources. This one comes from Jean-Baptiste Besard, *Thesaurus Harmonicus* (Cologne, 1603) folio 143[v].

No. 15

In Nos. 16 and 17 the diapasons are tuned at F and D.

No. 16 contains many *barré* chords. The left-hand fingering has been added for the more difficult passages. The importance of holding the bass notes for their full value has already been emphasized, but it is of almost equal importance that notes in the other voices should also be kept sounding. Several books of instruction from the sixteenth and seventeenth centuries say that no finger should be lifted from its place on the frets until it is needed for another note. While not strictly true, this statement does show the importance that was attached to the maintaining of a continuous sound and, of course, in music of polyphonic structure, of keeping all the voices alive. Hold lines have been added.

No. 16

Lesson 7

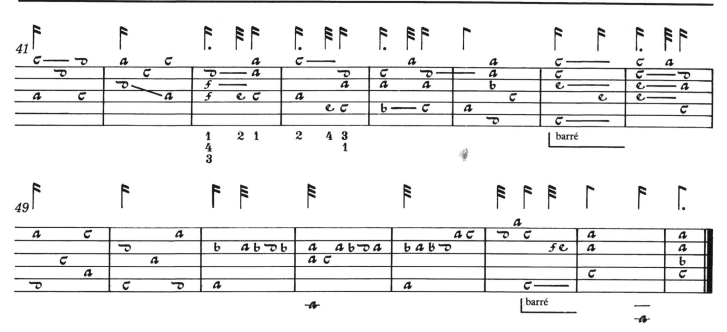

Courante.
Jacques Polonois

In No. 17 the marking for the diapasons is inconsistent and has been regularized. In bar 2 and bar 10 the jump to the letter *h* should be practised without looking at the left hand. In bars 17, 29 and 39 care must be taken that the bass notes continue to sound in the *barré* chords. The dotting for the right-hand fingering shows a mixed technique typical of the second decade of the seventeenth century during which time this manuscript was copied. The signs for graces are discussed in Lesson 16.

No. 17

Mall Simmes

Lesson 7

No. 18 comes from Thomas Robinson, *The Schoole of Musicke* (1603). Robinson uses a seventh course throughout the book, sometimes tuned at F, sometimes, as in the following piece, at D. In the tablature alphabet the letter *j* is omitted, so the last three notes of the final run will fall on frets 7, 9 and 10. If there are no frets higher than those tied on the neck of your lute it will be necessary to teach yourself exactly where to place the fingers on the soundboard so that these high notes will be in tune. When the left hand has to make a radical change of position, as in the penultimate bar, it is best, if possible, to make the jump on an accented note. In this case the *h* will be played by the thumb of the right hand.

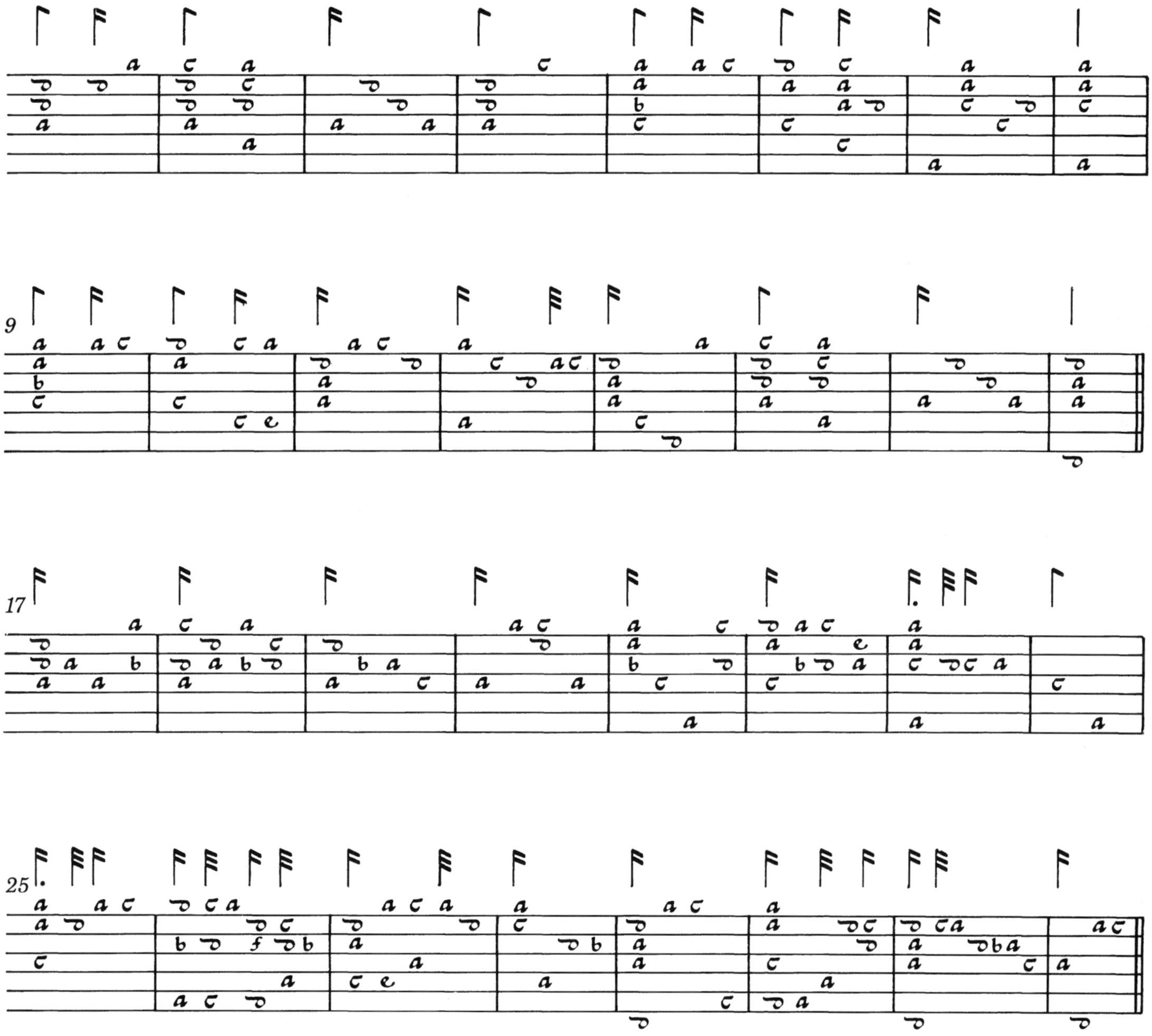

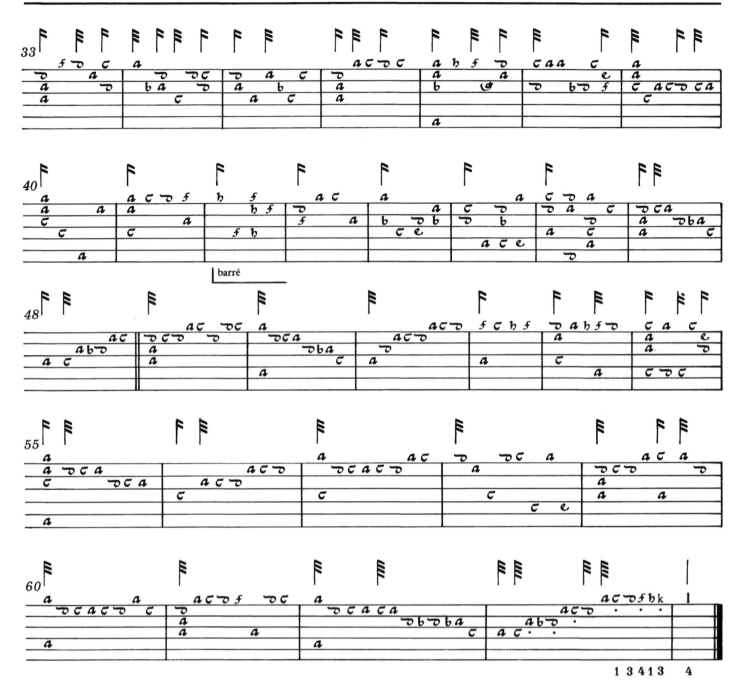

Go from my window

Lesson 8

All four of these pieces are excellent exercises for acquiring speed in playing rapid passages of single notes.

No. 19. Diapason at D.
The left-hand fingering for the changes of position on the high frets should again be followed carefully. Note also that in bar 2, when the first finger of the left hand is placed on the letter *h* it should remain in position together with the letter *k* until the *l* has been played when both these should be lifted together for the return to *h*.

Lesson 8

No. 19

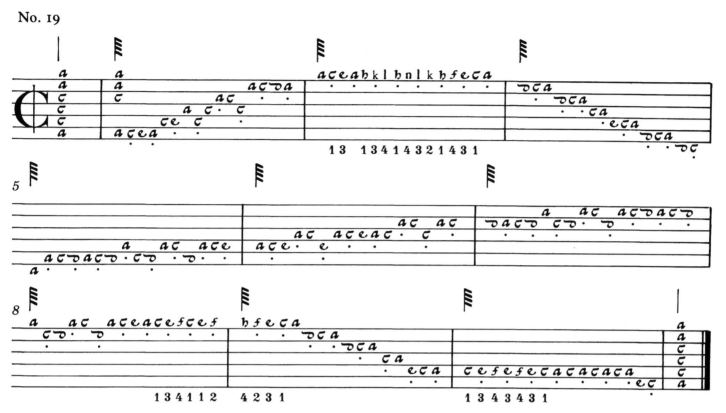

Passaggio

No. 20. Diapason at D.

In bars 5 and 8 it may seem, at first sight, a long stretch to take the letters c, d, f and h with the first, second, third and fourth fingers of the left hand. However, if the thumb is held lightly enough, it can follow under the hand up the neck of the lute, until, when the fourth finger is placed on h, it will be under the third finger, which at that point will be on the letter f. This position should be maintained while the h is played and then moved back when the second finger is placed on d.

No. 20

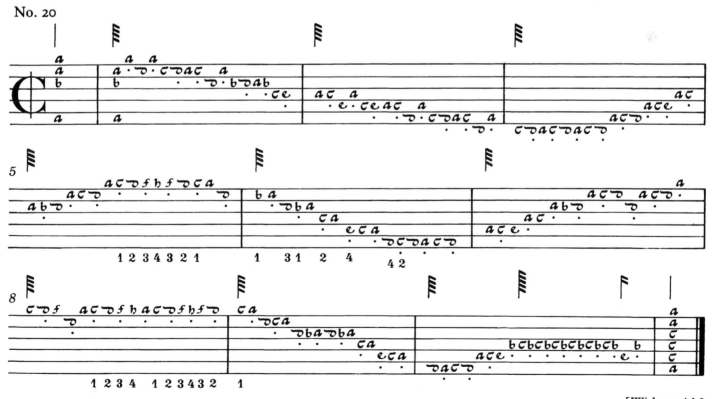

[*Without title*]

No. 21. Diapason at D.
The jump to the letter *h* in bar 3 should, by now, have been memorized and there should be no need to look at the left hand. The high passages are played with the same type of fingering as in No. 20.

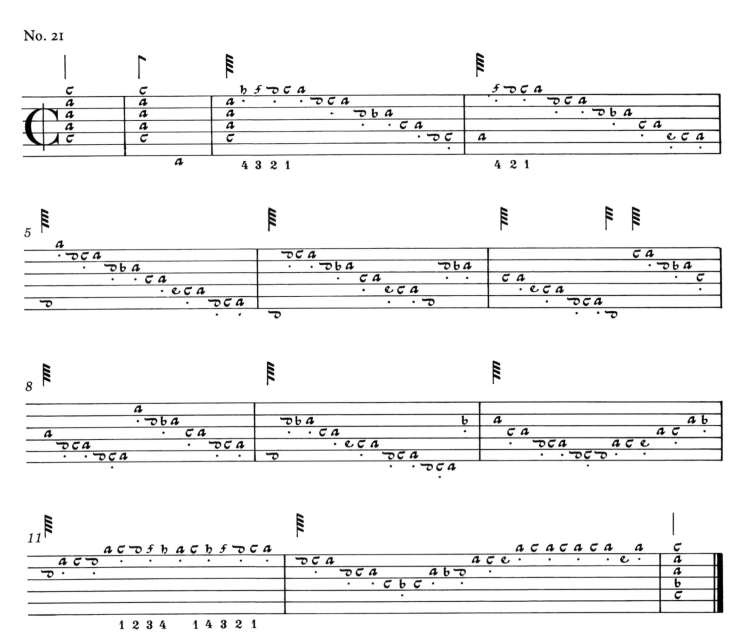

Passaggio

No. 22. Although the fingering dots for the right hand do not appear in the original, Jean-Baptiste Besard makes it clear in his *Thesaurus Harmonicus* (Cologne, 1603) that this is the type of right-hand fingering he recommends for rapid passages of single notes.* The last four notes in bar 2 should be played with the same movement in the left hand as described for the letters *h*, *k*, *l* and *h* in bar 2 of No. 19; then, without looking, the fingers 4 3 1 should be placed simultaneously on the letters *f*, *e*, and *c*. There are many groups of notes where the first finger must be kept in position. As a reminder these are marked 1————1.

*See 'Necessary Observations' translated into English in Robert Dowland, *Varietie of Lute-Lessons* (1610).

Lesson 8,9

No. 22

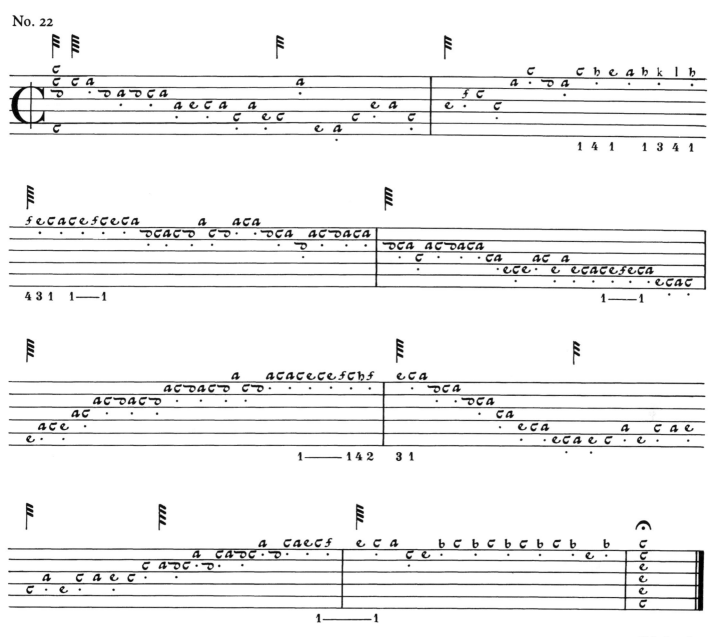

Diminutio.
I.B.B.

At this point, if you have not already done so, it is useful to begin to memorize the pieces. If you should become a professional player there are occasions in the theatre or television studio when you will be required to play without the music.

Lesson 9

Early French tablature was printed on a five-line stave. The Prelude which follows comes from Pierre Attaingnant, *Tres breve et familiere introduction* (Paris, 1529). The vertical lines have no other meaning, at this period, than to connect the notes of a chord or to link the time-mark with a single note. The use of capital letters placed on the lines was soon abandoned.

No. 23

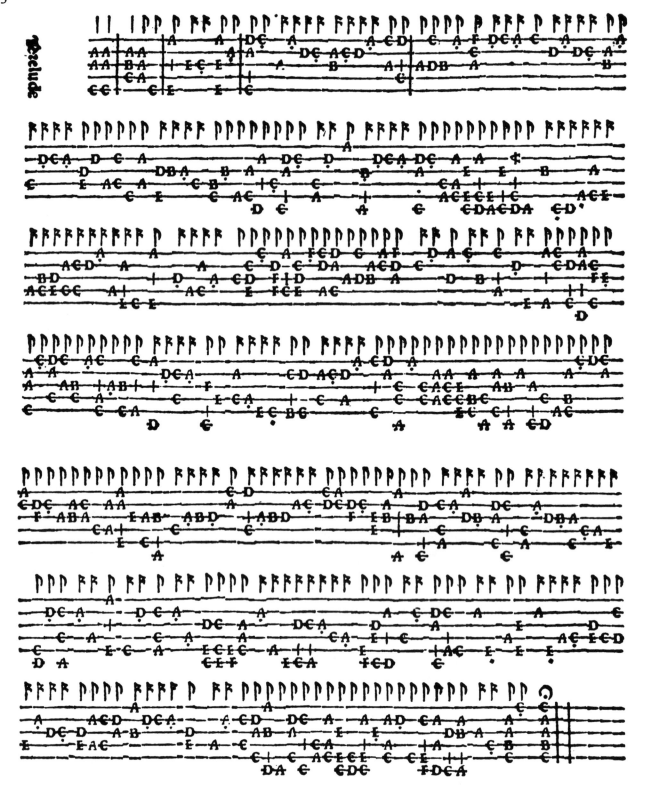

No. 24. This Fantasie, which comes from Albert de Rippe, *Premier Livre de Tabulature de Leut* (Paris, 1552) is typical in appearance of much of the lute music printed in France and the Netherlands during the middle years of the sixteenth century. The five-line stave was gradually replaced by the six-line stave and, by the end of the century, had dropped out of use altogether. The dots placed beside a chord indicate that the notes are to be played without the thumb.

Lesson 9

No. 24 FANTASIE

D'ALBERT.

Lesson 10

Here are a few entirely non-musical exercises for the development and control of the left hand which can be practised at odd times when the use of an instrument is not practicable.

1. Lay the left hand on the table with the thumb lying flat and the fingers arched, with the top joints as nearly vertical as possible. With one finger after another tap the table several times, the objective being to produce an even sound from each finger while the others remain completely still. The third and the little finger will prove difficult at first, but the muscles will gradually be brought under control.

2. With the hand still lying on the table in the same position, but with the fingers flat, starting with the first finger, pull each one upwards and backwards so that the lowest joint rises above the horizontal position of the back of the hand. Eventually it will be found possible to pull these joints back far beyond any position that is needed in the everyday movements of the hand, but muscles which are not normally used will have to be trained.

3. It is essential to achieve a wide stretch between each finger and, on a well-trained hand, it should be possible to obtain sufficient flexibility so that, without any sense of strain, the fingers may be pushed apart to the extent of a right angle. Start by stretching out the fingers, one after another, as far as they will go, then with the thumb and first finger of the right hand, gently push them apart a little further, but care must be taken not to press hard enough to cause any pain.

Lesson 11:
Italian tablature

A very large proportion of Renaissance music is written in Italian tablature, including music by some of the greatest masters. It is therefore necessary to learn to read this form with ease. My long experience of teaching has convinced me that it is less of a problem to the student before the French form has taken too firm a hold on his mind. The longer the initial effort is put off the more difficult it becomes, but once mastered it presents no difficulties at all.

Like all tablatures it does not represent musical sounds but indicates the positions in which the fingers are to be placed on the courses. The two outstanding differences from the French system are:

1. The positions of the fingers are represented by numbers instead of letters. 0 is the open course, 1 the first fret, 2 the second and so on.

2. The position of the courses is shown the other way up; that is with the highest course on the lowest line of the stave and the lowest course on the highest line.

In one sense it is more logical than the French since, having the highest string shown on the lowest line, it represents the position of the courses when the lute is held on the player's knee. In the early stages of learning I believe it is very helpful to think of the relation of these positions to each other. On the other hand it is, of course, incongruous in showing ascending runs as descending in position on the stave, and descending ones as ascending.

Begin by playing these two scales: the first, G major, ascending from the open sixth course up to the open first, and then descending to the sixth course again, then the scale of C major ascending from the fifth course to the first and back again.

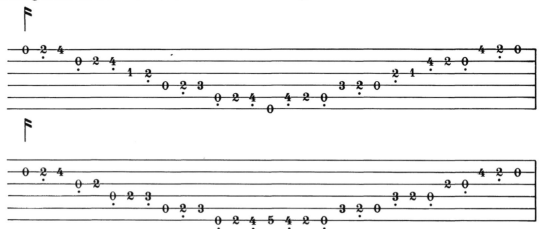

The following pieces are arranged in a series from very easy to slightly more difficult. Where a dot is placed under a chord it indicates that the notes are to be played without the thumb.

No. 25

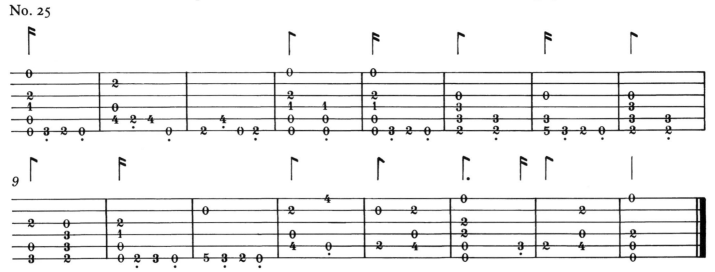

Pavaniglia

Lesson 11

No. 26

Contrapasso nuovo

No. 27

Misprints: *2 on 4; †2 on 5.

*Misprint: 0 on 6, 2 on 3, 3 on 2, and 2 on 1.

La rocha'l fuso

All through this piece the placing of the bar-lines is erratic and some marks are erroneously placed. In the only existing copy of this book, Julio Abondante's *Intavolature di Liuto*, 1546[1], some attempt has been made to correct these errors, not always very satisfactorily.

As included here the whole text has been corrected but the individual errors have not been separately noted.

No. 28

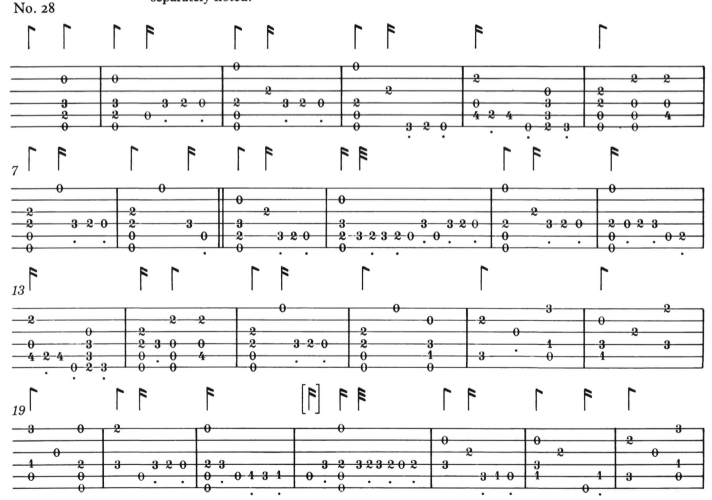

Lesson 11

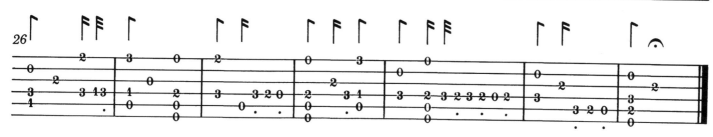

Zorzi Gagliarda

No. 29.   The following Balletto comes from Vincenzo Capirola's Lute Book (*c.* 1517) and in the instructions at the beginning of the book the importance of holding notes for the correct length of time is stressed. Two signs are used to show where a held note starts: ω , and where the finger has to be lifted: ᴖ . In bars 40 and 41 it is clear that it is 3 on the third course which has to be held; in bar 43 it is 2 on the fourth course and so on. In many of the early sources of Italian lute music a separate time-mark is placed over every note. Some of the pieces in Capirola's book have this type of marking. Others, as shown in the following pieces, only have a mark where the value of the note changes. In some of the pieces which follow the marking has been simplified.

No. 29

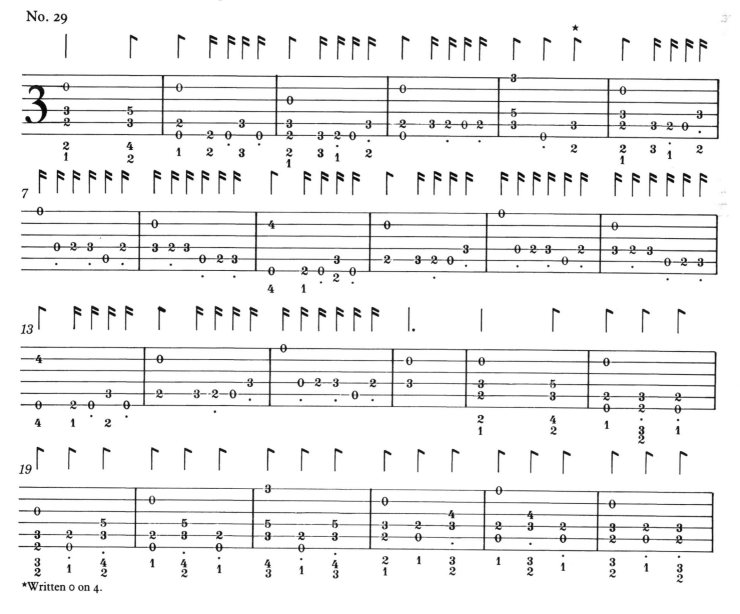

*Written 0 on 4.

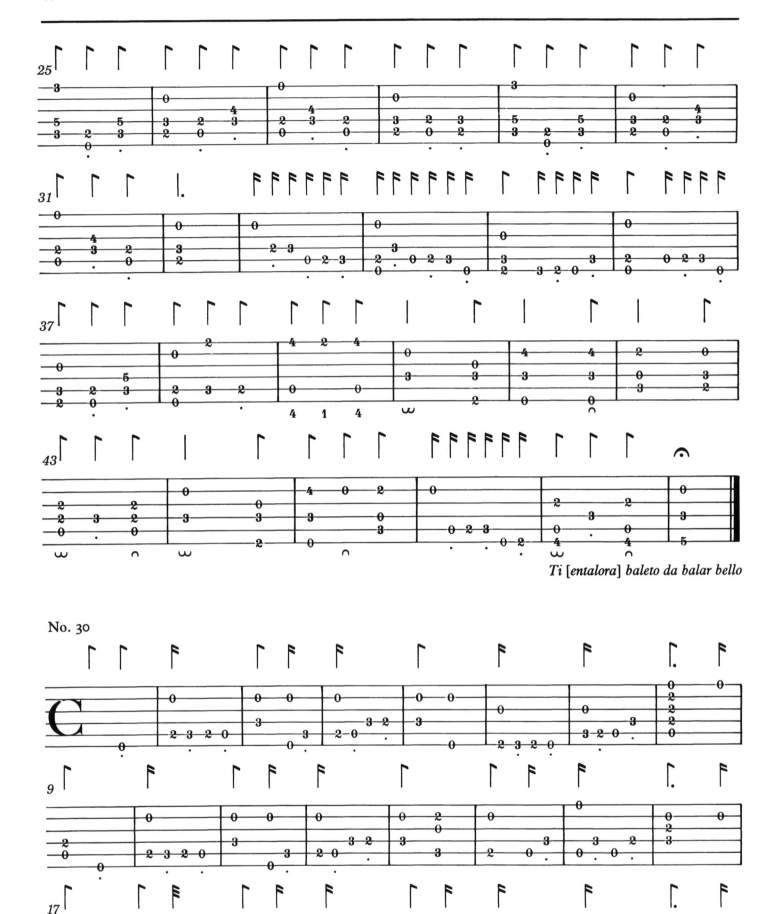

Ti [entalora] baleto da balar bello

Lesson 11

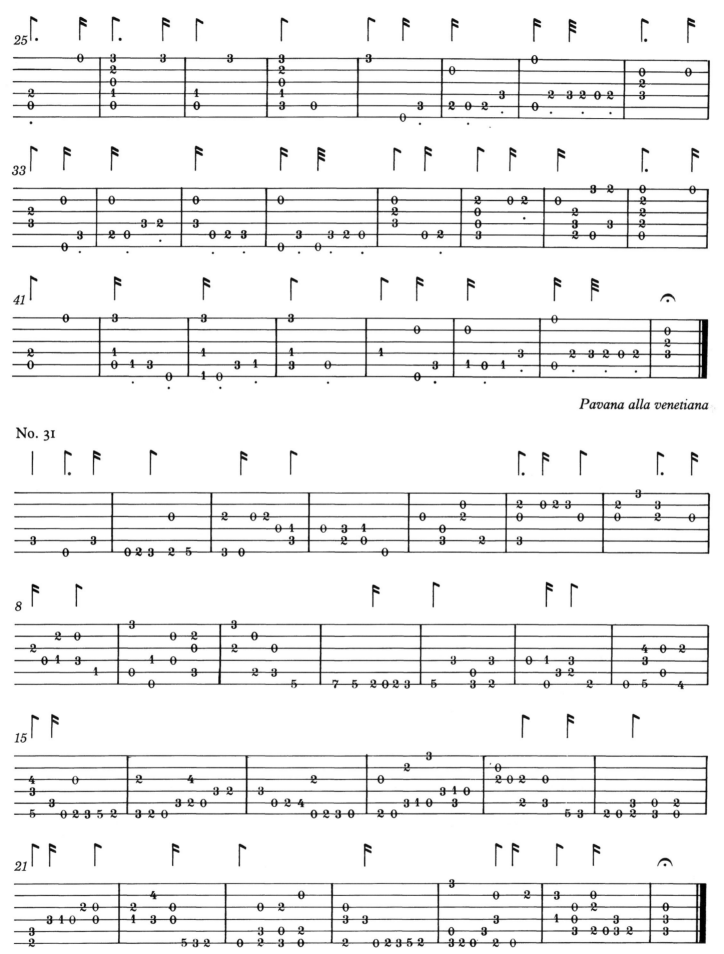

Pavana alla venetiana

No. 31

Fantasia de F. Milanese

No. 32. When a time-mark appears with no figure, or in the case of French tablature, no letter appears under it, it indicates that no note is to be played. In bars 6, 8 and 51 it shows that the preceding note is to be held. In bar 20, however, it is clearly a rest.

Lesson 11

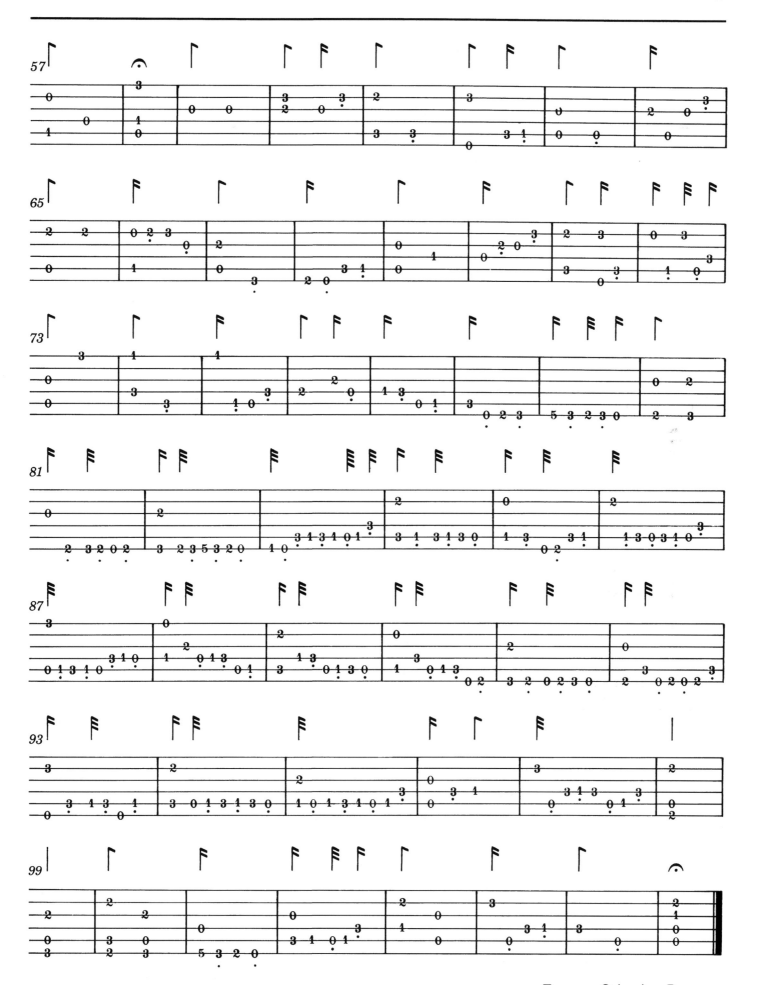

Francesco Spinacino, Recercare

No. 33   No. 33. Before a seventh course came into general use it was not uncommon to tune the sixth course down a tone, so that, as the instruction says, it becomes an octave with the fourth course.

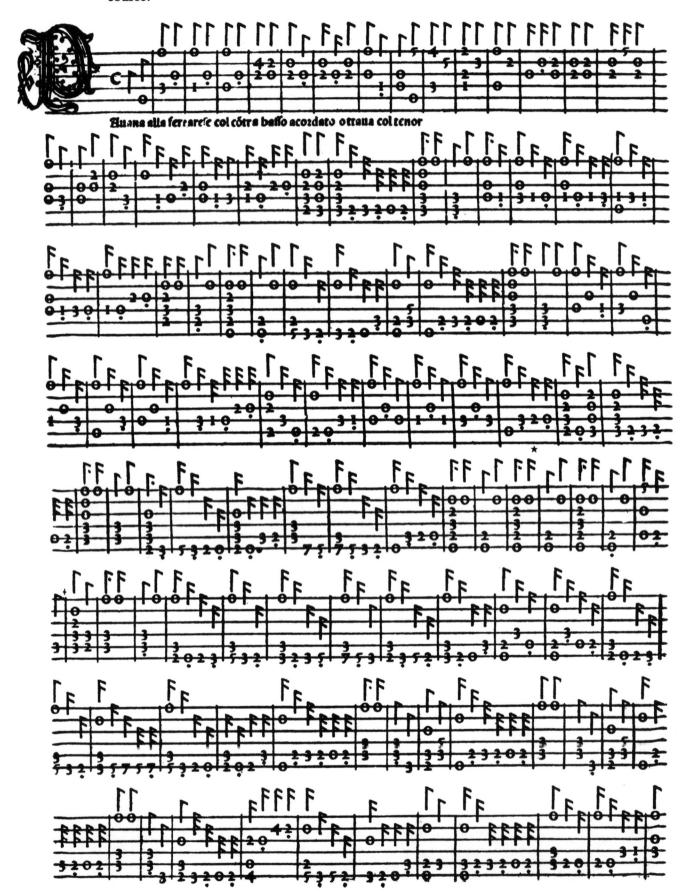

*Should be 1 not 2.

Lesson 11

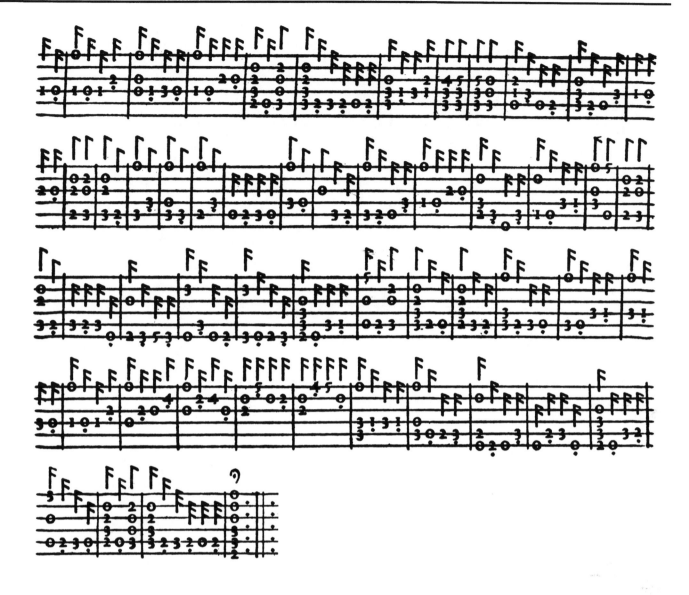

No. 34. The following Recercata comes from Book Two of Francesco da Milano's *Intavolatura de Viola o vero Lauto* (Naples, 1536). It is printed in the very rare form of tablature known as *Intavolatura alla Napolitana*: the stave is the same way up as in French tablature but the open course is numbered 1 and all the other frets are, therefore, one number higher than in ordinary Italian tablature. The 'viola' of the title refers to the flat-backed, waisted instrument, closely related to the Spanish vihuela.

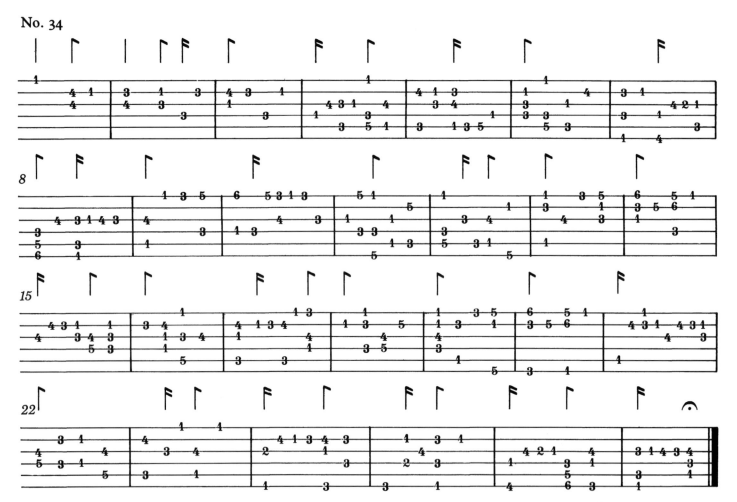

Recercata di Francesco Milanese

Lesson 12:
The hexachord

This was a system in which, unlike the later system of the octave, musical notes were grouped in a series of six. Guido d'Arezzo, in the eleventh century, called these notes *ut re mi fa sol la* from the initial syllables of a mediaeval hymn to John the Baptist:

Ut queant laxis
Re-sonare fibris
Mi-ra gestorum
Fa-muli tuorum
Sol-ve polluti
La-bil reatum
Sancte Iohannes.

Thomas Morley, in *A Plaine and Easie Introduction to Practical Musicke* (London, 1597), gives a very clear diagram of what, at the time, was called 'the Gam' or 'Gamut', showing how this system works.

As can be seen, each hexachord begins on one of three notes: the lowest starting on the G on the bottom line of the bass clef; the next on the C above; the next after that on the F above. These are repeated four times, counting upwards. The 'mutation' was brought about when the basic note series was moved from one hexachord to another. In this system the syllables *mi fa* had to be on a semitone interval. In the hexachord beginning on F therefore, the B had to be flattened. Thus the first accidental was introduced. The overlapping of the hexachords resulted in each note being defined by one, two or three syllables. In this way it was made clear in exactly which hexachord any note lay throughout the Gamut. For the singer a complication arose from the fact that when the voice moved out of one hexachord to another, the appropriate syllable of the hexachord into which it moved had to be used. This is shown by Morley in the following example which begins on the second hexachord and is written out in the tenor clef:

here transcribed into the treble clef and lowered an octave:

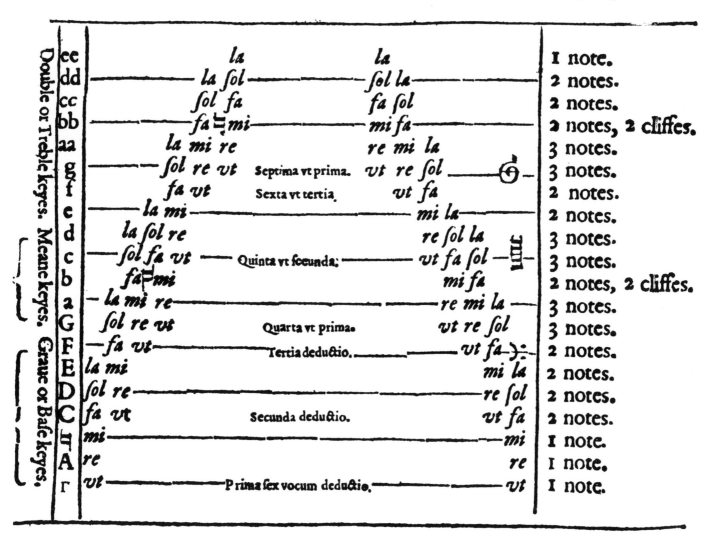

From: Thomas Morley, *A Plaine and Easie Introduction to Practical Musicke* (London, 1597)

Lesson 13:
Spanish music and the vihuela

Although all Spanish music of the kind that in other parts of Europe was written for the lute is described as for the vihuela,* there is ample evidence to show that the lute was extensively used in Spain in the sixteenth century and a number of compositions from the books of the

*The vihuela was a flat-backed instrument, guitar-like in shape, but with double strings on all six courses. They were made in several different sizes.

vihuelistas found their way into collections of lute music in other parts of Europe.* There seems no good reason, therefore, why, if the player does not possess a vihuela, the music should not be played on the lute.

The modes are often mentioned at the beginning of a composition, or indicated by signs and, theoretically, their finals should occur on the correct notes, nevertheless there is some evidence in the tuning instructions of the period that pitch was, to a certain extent, nominal and depended on how high it was possible to tune the top course without its breaking. It seems likely that, in fact, it was more a question of the placing of the intervals in each mode that determined the composer's choice and possibly, the convenience with which the notes would lie under the hand on the vihuela.

Although the existence of duos for which the instruments have to be tuned at different pitches is proof that more than one tuning was used, it seems clear that the case, argued by some players, that a large number of different instruments is needed in order to play all the compositions at their theoretically correct pitch, is not necessarily true.

The form of tablature used by Luys Milan uses numbers but it is the opposite way up from the usual Italian tablature and is shown in the following three pieces.

No. 35. This is an easy fantasia described as being in the first or Dorian mode which, in order to be theoretically correct, would require a vihuela in A. Luys Milan was a careful teacher and, if he wanted a piece played in a special way, he gave clear instructions. In this case no special directions are given but a transcription (35a) has been added here to show how the voices of the Fantasia must be held.

*See Diana Poulton, 'The Lute in Christian Spain', *The Lute Society Journal*, vol. XIX, 1977, p. 34.

Lesson 13

Fantasia del primero tono

No. 35a

Lesson 13

Fantasia del primero tono

In the following Fantasia, Luys Milan says the chordal passages should be played slowly and the running passages should be hurried. The *coronadas* indicate that a perceptible pause should be made.

Lesson 13

No. 36

Lesson 13

Fantasia II

In Spain, during the greater part of the sixteenth century, a wider range of strokes with the right hand was used than in any other part of Europe. The most comprehensive list for playing *redobles*, in this case meaning fast passages, is given by Venegas de Henestrosa in *Libro de Cifra Nueva para tecla, harpa y vihuela* (Alcalá de Henares, 1557), fol. 8^v:

1. *Dedillo*. The index finger alone moves upwards and downwards. (This is condemned by Miguel de Fuenllana, *Orphenica Lyra* (Seville, 1554, sigs. v^v and vi) as being imperfect because on the downward stroke the course is struck by the nail.)
2. *Figueta castellano* (Spanish *figueta*). The thumb crossing above (or outside) the index finger.
3. *Figueta extranjera* (foreign *figueta*). The index finger crossing above the thumb as generally used in the rest of Europe.
4. The alternate use of the second and index finger. (Fuenllana prefers this above all the others.)

Luys Milan includes some fantasias which, he says, are designed to be played with *dedillo* in the fast passages. Although this type of fingering is mentioned several times in Spanish sources no clear description is given. It appears to be a close descendant of the movement of the hand when the plectrum was held between the thumb and first finger, one of the positions sometimes shown in pictures of plectrum players. As with plectrum playing, the downward movement will be on the accented beat.

For the student who wishes to study this technique, with the very different sound that it makes, here is one of Luys Milan's fantasias specially written for the fast passages to be played in this way.

No. 37

Lesson 13

Fantasia del tercero y quarto tono

For the next exercise in *dedillo* playing we have to return to Italian tablature. The following piece comes from Alonso de Mudarra, *Tres Libros de Musica en Cifras para Vihuela* (Seville, 1546). He gives three signs to indicate the speed at which he wishes his compositions to be played:

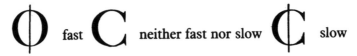

Dots between the lines simply show which notes are played together, or to which note the time-mark refers. They have no other meaning.

As can be seen he mixes *dedillo* with *dos dedos* using the contractions *dedi* and *dos de*. It is not entirely clear whether *dos de* means thumb and first finger or second and first finger since it was a common practice in Spain to number from the thumb to the little finger as 1 to 5. Miguel de Fuenllana distinguishes between these two techniques in the following way: thumb and first finger he calls *dedo pulgar y su companiero* and first and second fingers in our numbering he calls (in translation) 'the first two fingers of the four which are in the right hand'. Mudarra explains, in the instructions at the beginning of the book, that he uses *dedillo* on descending passages and *dos dedos* on ascending ones. There are, however, a few exceptions in some of the fantasias.

No. 38

Lesson 13,14
61

Fantasia de pasos largos para desemvolver las manos

Lesson 14:
More about Spanish music

The courses on the vihuela are numbered as follows:

Sesta
Quinta
Quarta
Tercera
Segunda
Prima

No. 39. The next piece comes from Luys de Narvaez, *El primero libro del Delphin* (Valladolid, 1538). In the instructions Narvaez gives the following signs for speed:

𝕆 somewhat fast   ₵ very slow

At the beginning of each piece he defines the tuning in words and uses two signs and to show on which courses the clefs of *ffaut* and *csolfaut* will fall (see p.51 for a diagram and explanation of the Hexachord). In this way the nominal pitch is indicated: F to f' for example, in the following piece. The signs and descriptions are, however, not always accurate.

In Spain *romances* and the *tonadas*, or melodies to which they were sung, appear to have been almost as well known as ballads and their tunes were in England. The subjects which mainly occupied the attention of the writers were stories about knightly deeds during the wars against the Moorish occupation, stories from the time of Charlemagne and stories drawn from classical and biblical history. The *tonada* to which 'Conde Claros' was sung is recorded in Francisco Salinas, *De musica libri septem* (Salamanca, 1577):

When collected and printed by Augustin Duran in *Romancero general* (1849-51) it began differently:

> Media noche era por filo,
> Los gallos querian cantar,
> Conde Claros por amores
> No podia reposar:
>
> (It was about the middle of the night,
> The cocks wanted to crow,
> Conde Claros for love
> Could not rest:)

It is an extremely long *romance* and tells the story of the love of Conde Claros for the beautiful Princess Claranina. In addition to Narvaez, Mudarra (1546) wrote eight *diferencias* on the *tonada*; Valderrabano (1547) one hundred and twenty; and Pisador (1552) thirty-seven.

The caption at the head of Narvaez's set reads in translation: 'The two lines show where each *diferencia* begins; they must be taken with a very slow beat to the bar'. The directions for the pitch of the vihuela say 'The second fret of the fourth course is *f fa ut*. The open second course is *c sol fa ut*.'

Tomás de Sancta Maria, writing in *Arte de Tañer Fantasia assi para Tecla como para Vihuela* (Valladolid, 1565) states that in order to play with grace it is necessary that the crotchets should be played in one way and the quavers in three ways. Of the crotchets he says you must pause on the first and hurry the second and he gives an example showing the first note as a dotted crotchet and the second as a quaver, and so on. Of the quavers he says the first way is to pause on the first note and hurry the second and he shows a passage written with dotted quavers and semiquavers. The second way is the reverse—to hurry on the first note and pause on the second. The third way is more elaborate and involves hurrying the first three notes and pausing on the fourth. He then makes it clear that with the crotchets and the two first methods with the quavers, the total value of the two notes should be preserved precisely. In the third method with the quavers, the second group must begin exactly on the half bar, that is, presuming the bar to have the value of four crotchets. He praises this method as being the most elegant of all, using the word *galano*.

No. 39

Lesson 14

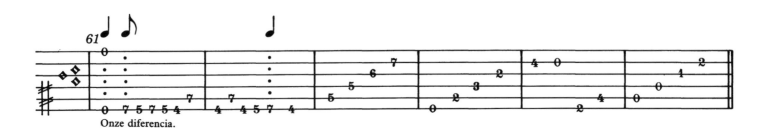
Onze diferencia.

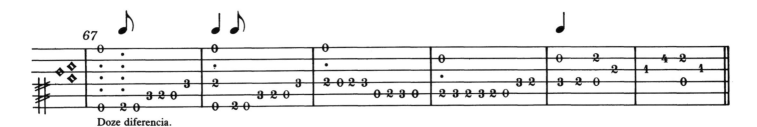
Doze diferencia.

Treze diferencia.

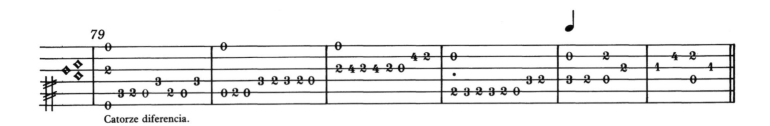
Catorze diferencia.

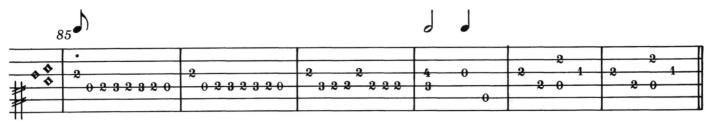
Quinze diferencia. Contra haziendo la guitarra.

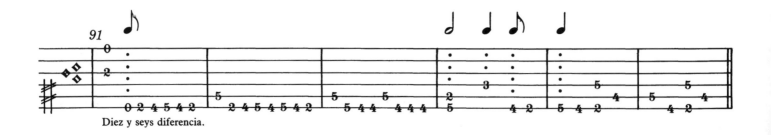
Diez y seys diferencia.

Lesson 14

Diez y sciete diferencia.

Diez y ocho diferencia.

Diez y novene diferencia.

Veynte diferencia. De proporcion seys minimas al compas.

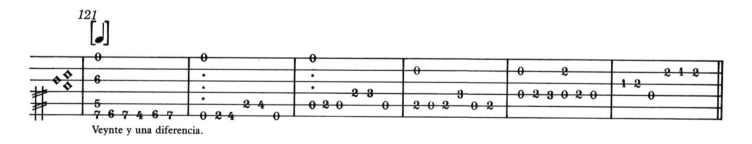

Veynte y una diferencia.

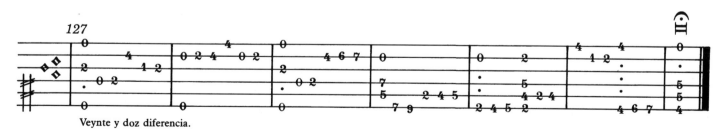

Veynte y doz diferencia.

Conde Claros del sesto tono

No. 40. In the following Fantasia by Miguel de Fuenllana I have suggested a possible way in which uneven quavers might have been used. As originally printed there is only a quaver time-mark at the beginning of each group. It is interesting to note that this Fantasia, on folio clxix[v] of *Orphenica Lyra* (Seville, 1554), is preceded by this remark:

Siguese una fantasia de redobles compuesta por el auctor, es de mucho provecho para desembolver las manos, y para tener alguna noticia de redobles galanos y de buena diminucion.

(Here follows a fantasia of *redobles* composed by the author which is very useful to loosen the hands and to have some knowledge of graceful *redobles* and of good diminution.)

Lesson 14

Fantasia de redobles

Questions

Here is a set of questions which the student working alone should ask him- or herself from time to time.

General questions
1. Are you holding the lute in such a position that the sound is being projected upwards and not downwards towards the floor?
2. Are you being careful not to look at either hand whilst playing?
3. Are you practising sight-reading in both French and Italian tablature and staff notation?
4. Are you beginning to memorize some of the pieces?

The left hand
1. Are you sure that no weight is being taken by the left hand?
2. Is the thumb being held freely enough so that it can slide backwards and forwards across the back of the neck of the lute and follow the hand when it moves upwards towards the rose?
3. Are the fingers being kept as nearly as possible at a right angle to the strings?
4. Are you being careful that the side of the hand is not being allowed to fall backwards towards the fret-nut, or even to touch the side of the peg-box?
5. Is the wrist being allowed to rise slightly when any of the fingers have to stop the sixth course so that it can be stopped with the tips and not with the front of the fingers?
6. When you have to hold a bass note, particularly in a *barré* position, can you hear the note sounding for the full length of time?

The right hand
1. Are you keeping the little finger steadily in position on the soundboard?
2. Are the fingers touching both strings of the course when playing all the courses?
3. Is the thumb striking downwards towards the soundboard and coming to rest on the course next to it wherever possible?
4. Are you carefully observing the alternating thumb and first finger, and second and first finger techniques where each one is appropriate?

Lesson 15:
Scales

Should you wish to take a diploma as either a performer or a teacher at a music college or conservatoire you may be required to play some scales. It is unlikely that you will be asked for keys with more than four accidentals, so here are major, and harmonic and melodic minor in those keys. They make good exercises in memorizing the exact position of all notes on the fingerboard. If you are not yet sure of where every note lies it is useful to write out each one in staff notation. You can, of course, if you wish to do so, take the exercise into more extreme keys. Scales can also be profitably used as exercises to increase technical agility.

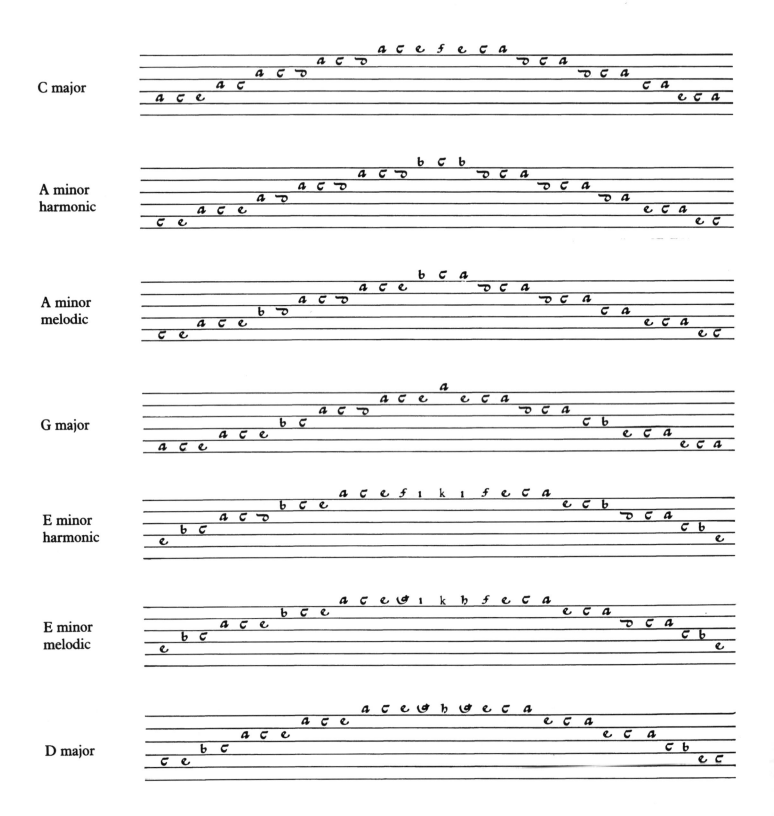

B minor harmonic

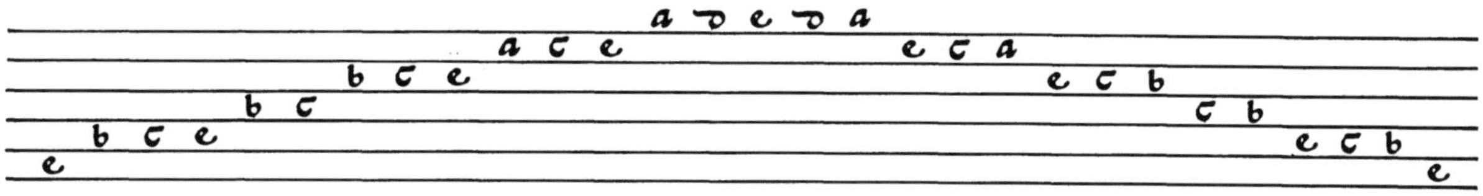

B minor melodic

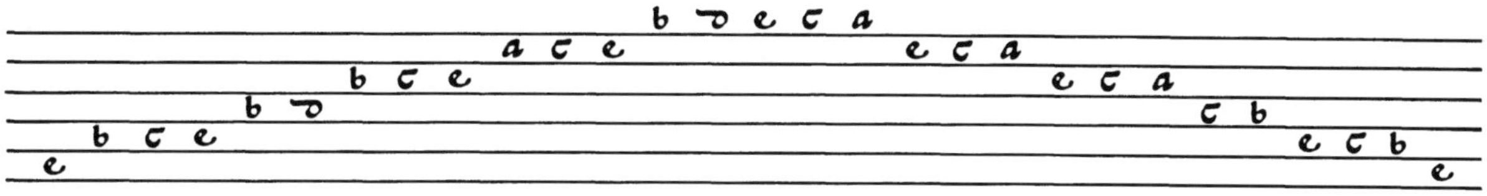

A major

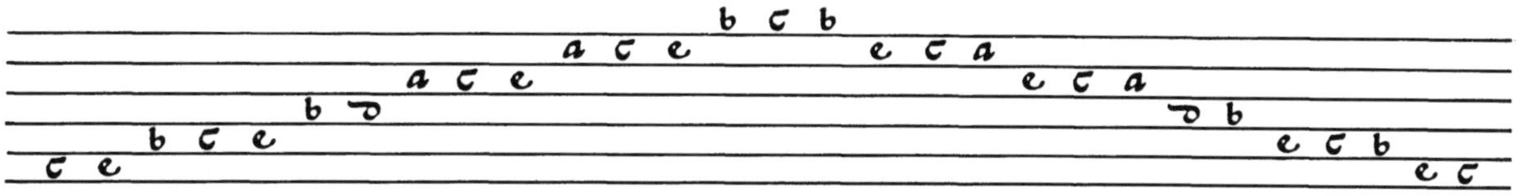

F sharp minor harmonic

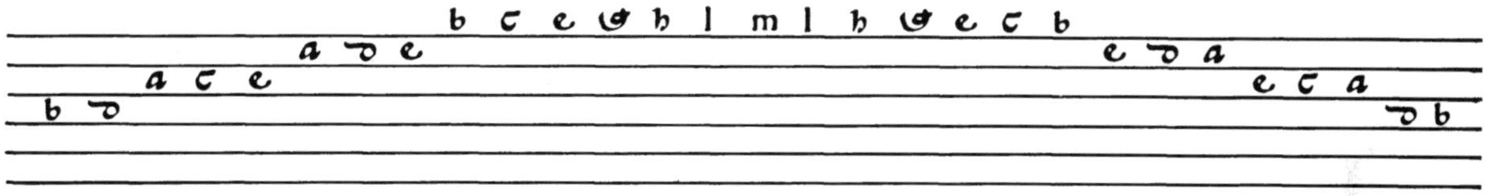

F sharp minor melodic

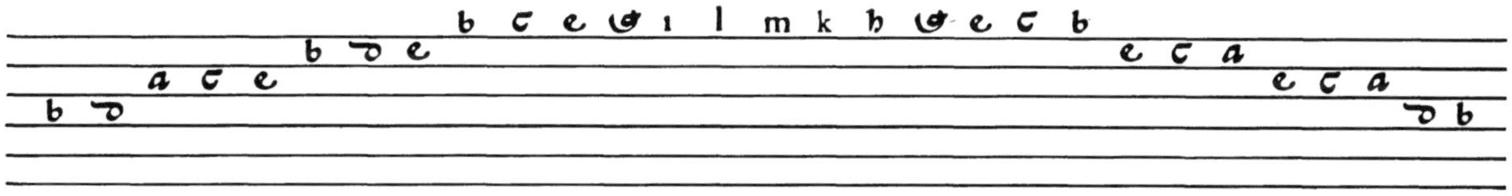

E major

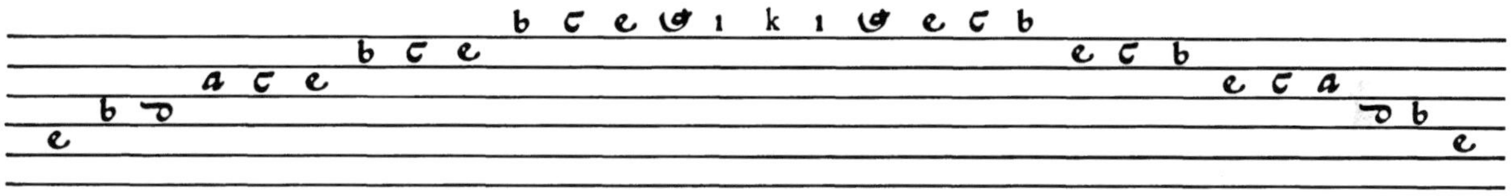

C sharp minor harmonic

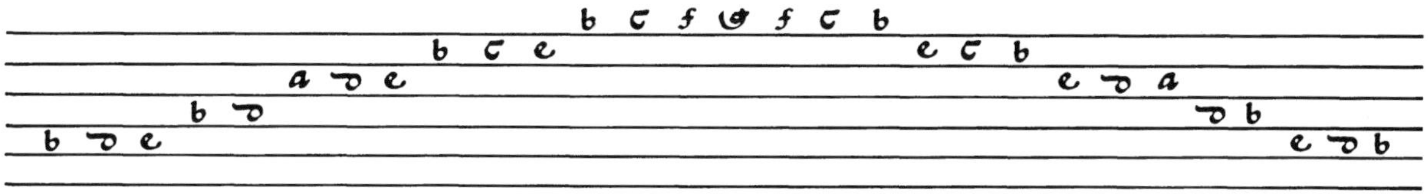

C sharp minor melodic

F major

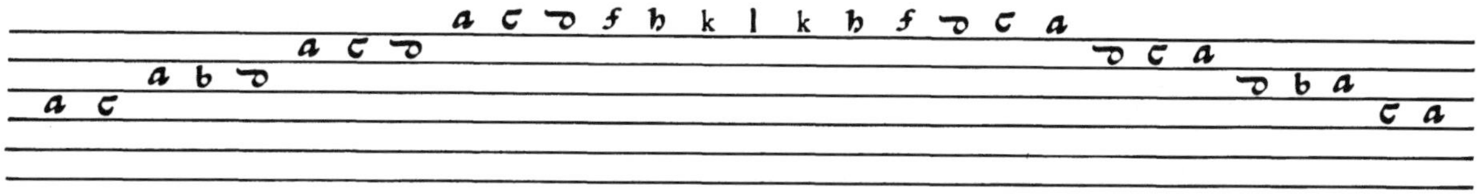

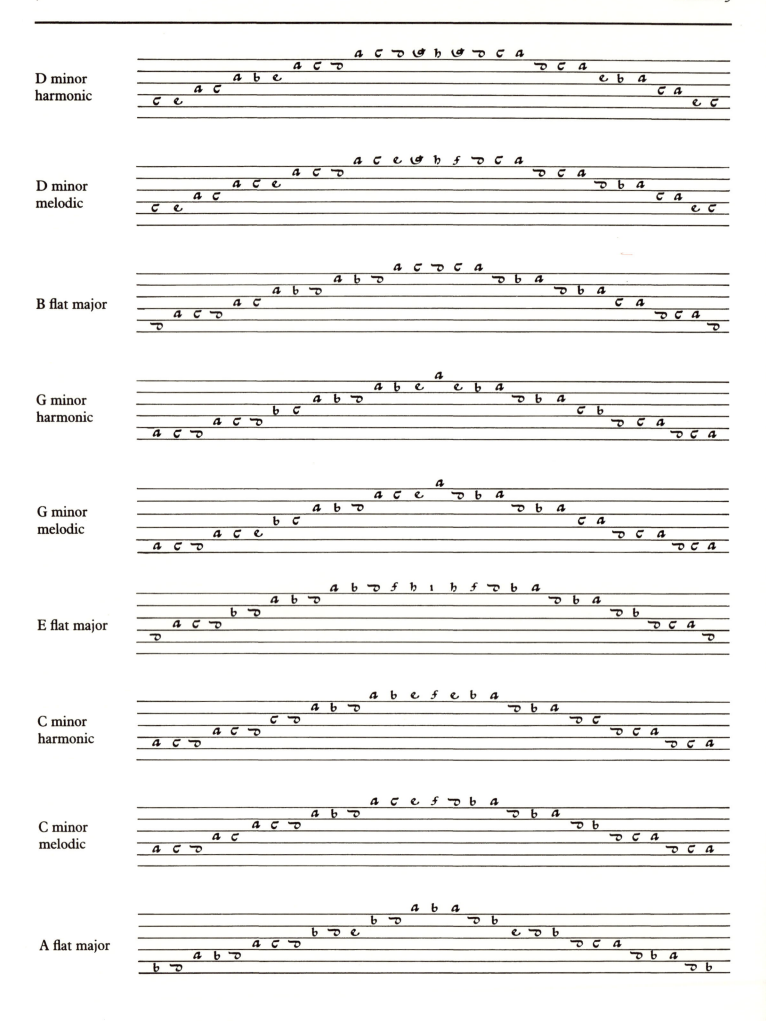

Lesson 16:
The use of graces in Renaissance lute music

A large number of sources that have come down to us provide evidence that additional decorative notes, played with the left hand alone and known in England as 'graces', were universally used. Although signs for graces appear in some of the earliest manuscript and printed books and their names are often mentioned, there are comparatively few lute books which give exact information as to how they are to be performed. For this reason it has been necessary to examine books of instruction for other instruments and vocal music to see whether any pattern of agreement can be found. What emerges clearly from this search is that not only did fashion change from country to country but also from period to period. Some composers too, show distinct preference for the use of particular graces.

It is clear from all the evidence that the use of graces was an accepted tradition and, even where no mention is made or no signs are included in the source being used, they should be introduced in the appropriate places. The fact that some manuscripts show no signs is probably due to the fact that the copyist felt it unnecessary to write them as he or she would supply them naturally in playing. Their absence in printed music is explained by Marin Mersenne in *Harmonie Universelle* (Paris, 1636) when he remarks that, in many cases, the printers do not have the appropriate signs in their shops.

The use of the term Renaissance as it occurs in the title of this book, in this particular context is very loose. It does not cover a period of time but is used to denote a particular style in the use and performance of certain graces and to exclude a change of fashion which showed itself in the lengthening of the appoggiatura, the disuse of certain graces and the introduction of others which came to be associated with the Baroque style. These changes, of course, came about gradually both in the nature of the individual graces and, as will be seen later, in the times at which they appeared and disappeared in various countries. Thus evidence suggests, for example, that the short appoggiatura was still normal practice in England for some time after it had been lengthened on the continent to half the value, or more, of the main note.

To give a performance of any piece in a manner as authentic as possible it is, therefore, necessary to give serious study to period, country of origin and, where expressed, to the taste of the individual composer.

On the lute the added graces are confined to those that can be played with a finger or fingers of the left hand alone after the initial stroke has been made with the right hand. For this reason some of the more elaborate graces such as the one which later became known as the 'shake turned':

are impossible to execute with the left hand alone, but are often written into the tablature as a decoration or diminution.

A study of sources where signs for graces are added shows that their use was spread across the courses from the first even down to the seventh. Where they are described it is generally implied that the added note must be within the key.

The graces, for which there is evidence to prove that they were used during the period that concerns us here, are as follows:

Appoggiatura from above:

Appoggiatura from below:

Mordent:

Inverted or upper mordent:

Shake from the note above the main note:

Shake starting on the main note:

'Slide':

'Fall with a relish':

Described by Tomás de Sancta Maria in *Arte de Tañer Fantasia assi para Tecla como para Vihuela* (Valladolid, 1565). Later called a 'turn':

Vibrato used strictly as a grace.

The earliest source of information about graces in lute music to have come to light so far is the Capirola manuscript (*c.* 1517). Vitale (or Vidal as he wrote it), a pupil of Capirola's and a great admirer of his work, decorated the pages of his manuscript and added prefatory notes in the hope of thus ensuring its preservation. Two signs are used: a figure in red dots following the main note, and two red dots placed over the main note. The descriptions, however, leave a considerable amount of uncertainty in interpreting their meaning. The antiquity of the language and the Venetian dialect add to the difficulties. In looking for help in an attempt to understand two key words I have gone to John Florio's *Queen Anna's New World of Words* (1611), since it appears to be the earliest comprehensive Italian-English dictionary, although of course it is nearly a hundred years later than Capriola's date.

The word *tremolizar* does not appear in either Florio or a modern dictionary, the nearest equivalent in each case being *tremare* 'to tremble, shake, quiver'. If this were taken literally it would suggest a vibrato but clearly, in this case, since other notes are involved, it cannot be so and must mean a movement of a left-hand finger on and off, or off and on, the string. The other word which is confusing is *al*, as the meaning, according to Florio, can be 'to the' or 'from the'.

The meaning then, of the explanation of the first sign, '*ti asegno tu dai una bota sul canto al 2° tasto tien ferma quella bota, et con uno altro deo tu tremolizi al terzo tasto . . .*' could be translated (as Otto Gombosi gives it in his edition of this book) 'let us assume that you make a beat on the second fret of the highest string; hold fast to this beat and tremolize with another finger on the third fret . . .'. If a more precise meaning had been in Vidal's mind when he wrote this sentence it could have meant that the grace started either on the main note or on the upper auxiliary.

Here is one example of how it appears in the text:

Except in the case of dance forms of which the steps are known, it is difficult to be sure of the exact speed at which any particular piece should be played. Even in Spanish sources where signs are used for 'fast', 'slow' or 'neither fast nor slow', and Luys Milan uses terms such as *apressurado* and *espacio*, our ideas of exactly how fast or how slow are bound to be, to a certain extent, subjective. Four ⌐ signs in a bar does not postulate any exact speed and, in a quick tempo, the above example could leave time for no more than a fall from above or, at most, an inverted mordent. Possibly on a longer note, as in the following example, a shake beginning either on the main note or the upper auxiliary could be used:

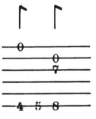

The second sign—the two dots placed over a note—is described as 'to tremolize with a single finger' and 'to tremolize on a single note'. Again I think the interpretation of these instructions would depend on the tempo of a four ⌐ sign passage. At a fast speed there would only be time for a mordent:

At a slower tempo, or in a passage such as the following:

it could be a repeated mordent, such as is shown is Elias Nicolas Ammerbach, *Orgel oder Instrument Tabulatur* (Leipzig, 1571), in Michael Praetorius, *Syntagma Musicum* (vol. III, Berlin, 1619), and as described by Thomas Mace in *Musick's Monument* (1676) where it is called a 'Beate'.

The appoggiatura

Intavolatura di Lauto del Divino Francesco da Milano et dell'Eccellente Pietro Paulo Borrono (Milan, 1548) appears to be the first book to show appoggiaturas carefully printed with the appropriate sign to mark their presence. Only the appoggiatura from above is used. The directions say that the grace is to be played on the beat and should take the accent as if it were the main note. (See composition No. 42.) Tomás de Sancta Maria gives both forms and adds that the one from above (*fa mi*) should be used in ascending passages and the one from below (*sol fa*) in descending ones. This may have been the fashion in Spain at the time but the rule does not seem to apply in other countries.

There is one point of importance that should be noted. In England, right up to the time of the publication of Henry Purcell's *The Harpsichord Master* (1697), when it was written out in lists of graces, the appoggiatura was shown as one quarter of the value of the main note:

The long appoggiatura seems not to have been mentioned in England until Charles Dieupart's *Suites de Clavecin* was published in London without date.* In the table of graces, in French and English, the appoggiaturas are shown as half the length of the main note. Meanwhile on the continent they began to change their length considerably earlier. Michael Praetorius, in *Syntagma Musicum* (vol. III, Berlin, 1619), says the appoggiatura takes one third of the length of the main note, and Marin Mersenne, in *Harmonie Universelle* (Paris, 1636), says it takes half its value. A method of playing an appoggiatura from below, which seems unique to this composer, appears in Pietro Paolo Melii, *Intavolatura di Liuto Attiorbato*, Libro Secondo (Venice, 1614), where he shows the two figures ⌒4⌒5 and adds 'where you find the ligature above strike the first and glide with the same finger onto the second which is the main note'.

The mordent and the inverted mordent

The mordent seems to have been widely used and is mentioned in a number of treatises. The possibility of its use by Capirola has already been mentioned. Tomás de Sancta Maria says it should be used on ascending passages but again this may have been a local fashion or a personal preference. Although Mace is the only English lutenist to describe it, it is included in the table of graces in the Manchester Lyra Viol Book (*c.* 1650).

The inverted mordent may have been used by Capirola as has already been discussed. Tomás de Sancta Maria, on the other hand, shows it clearly in notation and says it is used in descending passages. Evidence suggests that it maintained its popularity in Spain up to the time of the printing of Pablo Nassare's *Escuela Musica*, Secunda Parte, Libro Quarto (Zaragoza, 1724, p. 470), where it is clearly explained in terms of keyboard fingering. Outside Spain there is less evidence of its use during the Renaissance period. Girolamo Diruta, in *Il Transilvano Dialogo sopra il vero modo di Sonar Organi, & istromenti da penna* (Venice, 1593 and 1597), shows the following example under the heading *Tremoli sopra il Seminime*:

---

*See Arnold Dolmetsch, *The Interpretation of the Music of the XVII & XVIII Centuries* (London, 1916), p. 122. The date suggested is 1715-25.

Lesson 16

and Michael Praetorius, in *Syntagma Musicum* (vol. III, Berlin, 1619, p. 235), under the heading *Tremoletti*, gives the following example on an upward passage:

It is not mentioned in Marin Mersenne's extensive list of graces and I have been unable to find any other evidence of its use in France.

In England it does not appear in any tables of graces, nor does it agree with any verbal description. There is a possibility, however, and it must be emphasized that this is no more than conjecture, that one of the signs in a manuscript in the British Library, Add. MS 38539, indicates this grace. The single cross stands for a grace involving a lower auxiliary and the double cross, which occurs on both long and short notes, for one involving an upper auxiliary. The third sign, 7, occurs, with few exceptions, in descending passages and could indicate an inverted mordent:

In the Boethius Press facsimile edition of *The Board Lute Book* (Leeds, England, 1976) Robert Spencer suggests that one of the signs used by Margaret Board could also have had this meaning. Nevertheless, with so little evidence to go on, I think this grace should be used with caution.

Shake from the note above the main note Tomás de Sancta Maria, on folio 48, writes out his shake beginning on the main note but he adds that it is now the fashion to begin it on the note above the one on which it finishes. From then on, until Henry Purcell, who says in his *The Harpsichord Master* (1697) 'observe that you allwayes shake from the note above', it seems to have been the more general practice to begin the shake on the upper auxiliary. There are, however, exceptions to this, as shown below.

Shake beginning on the main note Girolamo Diruta, *Il Transilvano* (Venice, 1593 and 1597) describes the *Tremolo* as a short shake beginning on the main note, although in some of his diminutions he writes out a shake beginning on the upper note. Elias Nicolas Ammerbach, *Orgel oder Instrument Tabulatur* (Leipzig, 1571), shows a short shake. In Michael Praetorius's *Syntagma Musicum* (vol. III, Berlin, 1619) the *Tremolus Ascendens* is a short shake. In Thomas Mace's *Musick's Monument* (1676) both the 'Hard' and 'Soft' shake are described as beginning on the main note.

The slide This name is given in the table of graces on folio 32ᵛ of The Board Lute Book and the sign is a slur. As Robert Spencer points out in his notes, it occurs on the letters *acd* and *eca*. The first of these is called an 'Elevation' and the second a 'Double Backfall' by Christopher Simpson in *The Division Violist* (1659). In the Manchester Lyra Viol Book (c. 1650) they are called 'A fall' if it is a minor third, 'An Elevation' if it is a major third, and 'A double back-fall'. Thomas Mace calls the ascending form 'a whole fall' and says it can be either a major or minor third. Christopher Simpson and Thomas Mace write of it respectively as 'now somewhat obsolete' and 'much out of use in these our days'. It is impossible to estimate how long such a change of fashion takes to establish itself but in the table of signs in the part of The Board Lute Book in which Margaret signs herself by her married name (according to Robert Spencer her marriage took place between the years 1623 and 1631) no mention is made of its being out of date and it can probably be used in music of the Jacobean period without misgiving.

A fall with a relish

Thomas Robinson, in *The Schoole of Musicke* (1603) describes three graces:
  1. A 'fall'. This comes from below the main note and can be either a tone or a semitone according to the key.
  2. A 'relish'. Although he does not describe exactly how this is performed, either a shake or an appoggiatura from above seems to be implied.
  3. A 'fall with a relish'.

The combination of an appoggiatura and a shake is described by Marin Mersenne but is not given a name and Matthew Locke, in a table of graces on page 5 of *Melothesia* (1673), lists 'a Fore-fall and Shake'.

Thomas Robinson has an interesting comment to make on the use of graces:

. . . and note that the longer the time of a single stroke, that the more need it hath of a relish, for a relish will help, both to grace it, and also to continue the sound of the note his full time: but in a quicke time a little touch or jerke will serve, and that only with the most strongest finger.

A turn

This grace is written out by Tomás de Sancta Maria but is not included in any book which describes graces for the lute. It was probably more generally associated with keyboard music and, since it is shown in the table of graces in the Manchester Lyra Viol Book, with bowed instruments. It is, of course, often found written out in lute music in the form of a 'shake turned' as in the following passage:

Vibrato

Luys Venegas de Henestrosa, in *Libro de Cifra Nueva para tecla, harpa y vihuela* (Alcalá de Henares, 1557), gives a clear description of vibrato. He says to '*menear* [to wriggle or shake] the finger on the string and fret you wish to play'. Nicolas Vallet, in a book of arrangements of psalm tunes, *Piètè Royale* (Amsterdam, 1620), makes frequent use of vibrato which he indicates with a double cross ⋇. Marin Mersenne calls vibrato '*verre cassé*' and has this interesting comment to make: 'As to the *verre cassé*, I am adding it here, although it is not used as much now as it was in the past, in as much as it has a very great charm when it is made properly. And one of the reasons why the moderns have rejected it is because the older ones used it almost all the time. But since it is as much a fault not to use it at all as to perform it too much, it must be used in moderation.' In spite of its early popularity as described by Mersenne, this is not an easy grace to perform effectively on the lute. The left hand must, at the moment the right hand strikes the string, be held so lightly that it can be shaken sufficiently to create the necessary movement of the string.

No standardized set of signs for graces existed in the period with which we are dealing here nor was any consistent use of names adopted. To interpret the signs therefore, note must be taken of whether they occur on long or short notes and whether they occur on open or stopped strings. In some cases only one sign is used—generally a double cross in English sources and a comma in French. In these cases it is left entirely to the player to decide which of those in use is best suited to the particular point in the music at which the sign occurs. If two are used, examination will generally show that one sometimes occurs on open strings and must, therefore, indicate a grace involving the upper auxiliary. The other sign will then indicate a grace involving a note below the main note.

In the lessons that follow, where signs for graces are used, an explanation of their probable meaning will be given.

Lesson 17:
The performing of graces

At this period evidence suggests that all graces are performed on the beat except in the case of Tomás de Sancta Maria who describes the first note of the shake as coming before the beat. He appears, however, to be thinking in terms of the keyboard and it is almost impossible to perform a shake in this manner on the lute where a chord is involved.

The following exercises will help to develop the ability to play graces clearly and with precision. Although the accent falls on the first note of the grace it must be remembered that the note or notes played with the left hand alone must have sufficient sound to be audible to the listener.

Exercise 1

In playing the appoggiatura from above, after the first note has been played with the right hand, the finger of the left hand which is stopping that note must be pulled off with a sideways movement—'a kind of a Twitch' as Thomas Mace calls it. This is not difficult except possibly at first, in the case of the fourth finger. It should stop the first note with the exact tip, with the top joint as nearly vertical as possible.

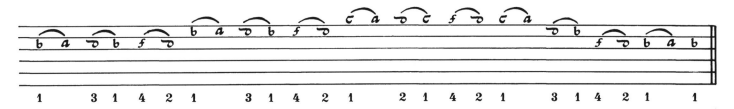

Exercise 2

The appoggiatura from below. In this grace, after the first note has been played with the right hand, the finger of the left hand beats down on the course to sound the note. Again it is the fourth finger which may, at first, be difficult to control so that it produces an adequate sound.

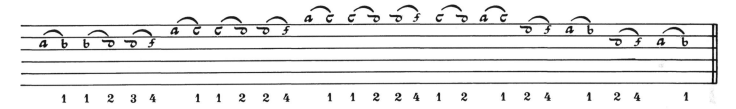

Exercise 3

Here it is necessary to be careful that the movement of the finger performing the grace does not disturb the finger holding the bass note or the sound will be killed.

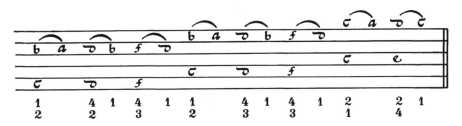

Exercise 4

The short shake is simply a repetition of the appoggiatura from above and again, care must be taken that the final note is clearly audible.

Exercise 5

In Exercise 3 listen for the continuing sound of the bass note, and in Exercise 5 of both bass and treble while the shake is performed.

Lesson 18

In this Ricercar from the Capirola manuscript both his signs for graces are used. (See p. 73 for a discussion of the possible meaning of the signs.) Take careful note of the sign ω for holding the finger in place, and ∩ for releasing it. Some left-hand fingerings have been added in square brackets where, in order to maintain the voices, an unusual choice has to be made and on chord changes where the fingers can be prepared for a chord following another before the first one has been played.

No. 41

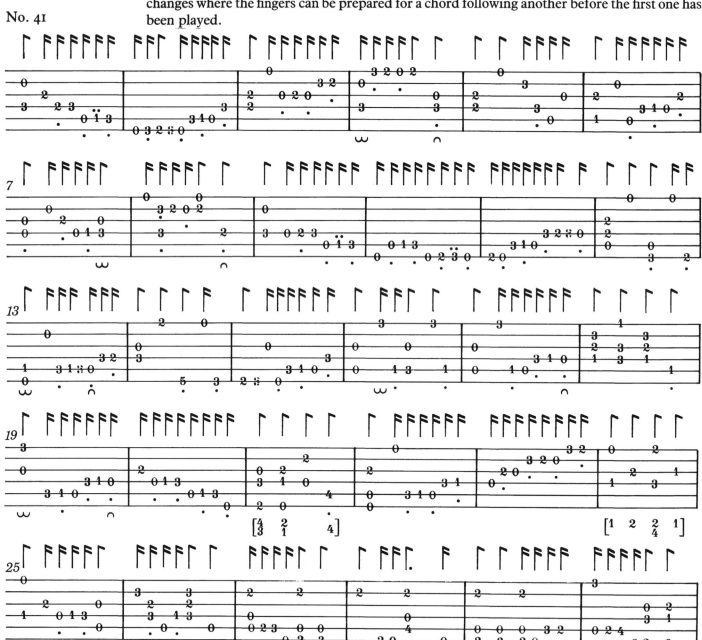

Lesson 18

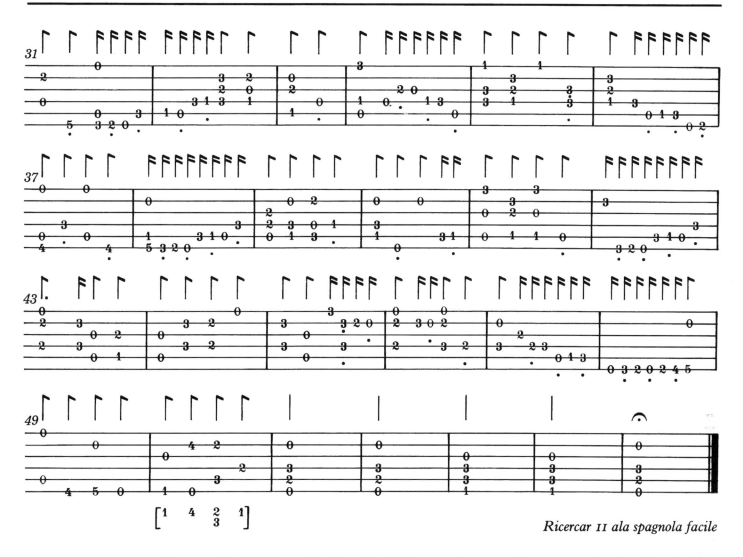

Ricercar 11 ala spagnola facile

No. 42. In this Pavana by Pietro Paulo Borrono the appoggiaturas must be played on the beat and the first note takes the accent. The small cross placed under a note shows that the note must be held.

No. 42

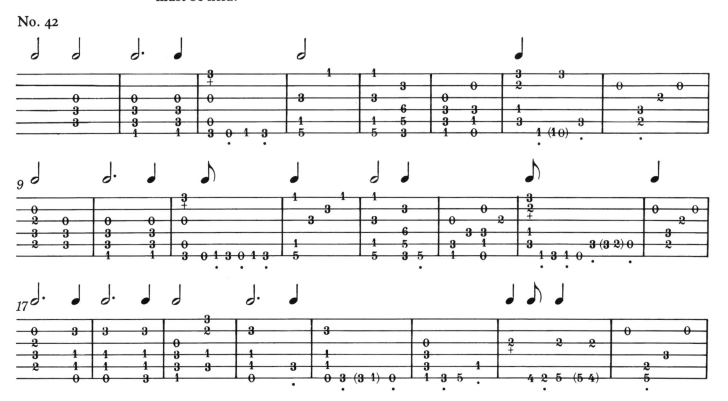

Pavana novissima detta la Lucretia

No. 43. Nicolas Vallet, in his *Paradisus Musicus Testudinis* (Amsterdam, 1618), uses two signs: a comma placed after the letter which indicates an appoggiatura from above, and a cross, which he says is 'similar to the preceding, but must be redoubled by pulling the course with the left hand two or three times'—clearly a shake. Although the piece is described as 'A 9' (i.e. for a nine-course lute), only the courses tuned at F and C are used.

No. 43

Lesson 18

Ballet

No. 44. Here is an example of how Nicolas Vallet, in his *Pièté Royale* (Amsterdam, 1620), uses the sign ✳ to indicate a vibrato. With gut strings this can be quite effective, but with nylon it is difficult to produce much change in the sound. This psalm is arranged for a ten-course lute with diapasons at F, E, D and C:

Psalm 58

Lesson 19:
Graces in English sources

The earliest English source containing signs for graces to which an exact date can be given is William Barley's *A new Booke of Tabliture* (London, 1596). Here only one sign, the double cross, is used. From about the turn of the century more signs begin to appear. Two are commonly used, though not invariably, to differentiate between graces involving an upper auxiliary and those involving one below the main note. As the seventeenth century progressed a greater variety of signs was introduced and the extent to which gracing was used also increased. Examination of some later sources suggests that in England the gracing of lute music was more highly cultivated than in any other European country.

No. 45. This piece by Francis Cutting from Barley's book shows how the sign is placed. No explanation of its meaning is given and it may indicate the same grace all the way through. In bar 4 it is clear that it must imply a grace using the upper auxiliary, perhaps an appoggiatura or a short shake. Where the graced note is preceded by a note below, however, as in bars 11 and 15, it is possible that it may mean an appoggiatura from below or a mordent. In the typeface used here, the top note of the first chord in bar 2 is *c*, and the second note in bar 3 is *e*. The piece comes from the section of Barley's book devoted to music for the orpharion, but there is nothing to distinguish it from lute music by Francis Cutting which appears in other sources.

No. 45

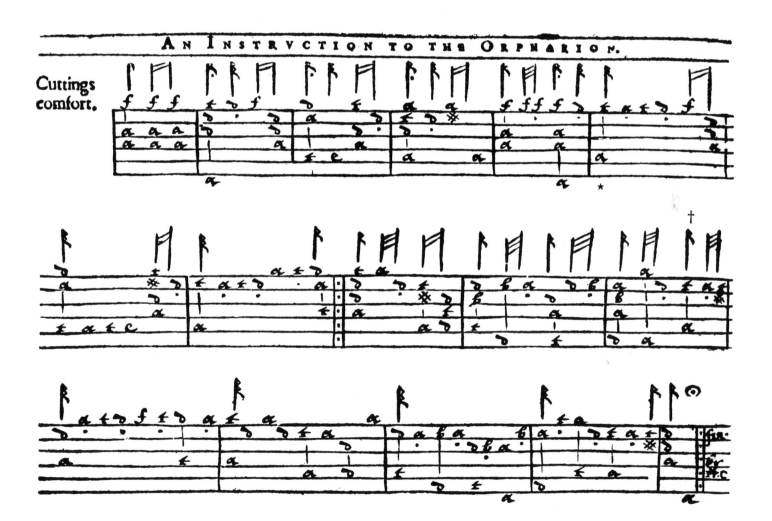

*Should be *a* on 4.   † Time-marks should probably be

No. 46. In this piece from the Weld manuscript (*c.* 1600) the following two signs are used and possible interpretations are suggested:
 ⊣ appoggiatura from below, mordent or slide
 ♯ appoggiatura from above or shake

No. 46

Watkins ale

Lesson 19 85

Nos. 47 and 47a. These two versions of John Dowland's 'Battle Galliard', later known as 'The King of Denmark's Galliard', come from the Folger Shakespeare Library, Washington, D.C., 1610. 1. (early sixteenth century), fols. 10ᵛ, 11, and London, British Library, Add. MS 38539. (c. 1615) fols. 12ᵛ, 13. They differ both from each other and from the version in *Varietie of Lute-Lessons* (London, 1610). Although the graces are used in a slightly different way in each manuscript, bar 17, and each time it recurs, is treated in exactly the same way. In No. 47, however, a greater variety of graces is used. Here are possible explanations:

♯ appoggiatura from above or shake
• appoggiatura from below ('fall'), slide or mordent
•♯ 'fall with a relish' as described by Thomas Robinson see p. 76

In both manuscripts the typical ꞇ (c) of the Secretary Hand is used, and the rather curious long-tailed sign for *h*.

In No. 47a two signs only are used, possible explanations being:

♯ appoggiatura from above or shake
x appoggiatura from below, slide or mordent

No. 47

Lesson 19

No. 47a

*This bass note is incorrectly marked with a single line.

Lesson 19   89

No. 48. This Fantasia by John Dowland also comes from Add. MS 38539, fols. 14ᵛ, 15. As with the previous piece it differs from the version in *Varietie of Lute-Lessons*. It is particularly interesting for the way in which the use of graces contributes towards an understanding of how the composition should be performed. Their lavish use down to half-way through bar 64 suggests a fairly moderate speed with, perhaps, a very slight *rallentando* on the last four notes. Then suddenly the whole character changes and down to bar 73 not a single grace appears and a rapid speed seems called for. In bar 74 a new section appears with a profusion of graces which suggests the return to a moderate speed down to bar 83. Again a burst of speed seems called for down to the final bar which could close the performance with a return to the original tempo.

No. 48

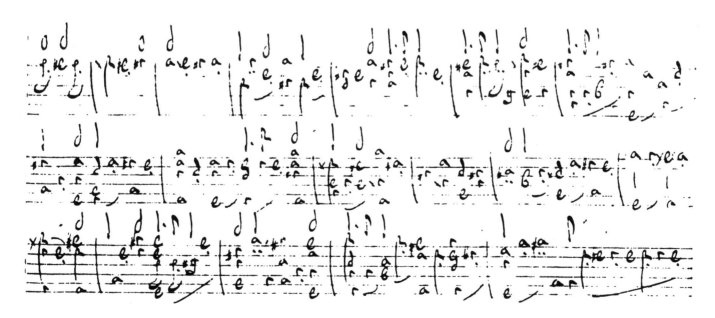

Lesson 19

No. 49. Of the eighty-nine compositions in Add. MS 38539 the sign 7 appears in twenty-two. There seems no perceptible pattern in which pieces the sign is used. It is not confined to the work of any special composer nor is it found consistently in every work of any composer. It appears in both the handwritings in which the pieces are written. The only characteristic shared by the various placings of the sign is that they generally occur on descending passages. In spite of the lack of evidence of its use in England, the possibility that it indicates an inverted mordent cannot be overlooked (see p. 74). Diapasons at F, E, D and C.

Allmayne by m^r Ro Johnson

The marking for the diapasons is rather curious in the original. The three strokes for the note C at the end of the first strain imply a ten-course lute but possibly the writer used them only to indicate the lowest course since the E natural in the penultimate bar is obtained by stopping the eighth course on the second fret. Even here it is incorrectly marked with two strokes which would indicate a ninth course. There is no reason why the note should not be played on the open ninth course tuned at E natural on a ten-course instrument.

No. 50. This Galliard by John Dowland, from the *Sampson Lute Book*, is a different version of the piece which appears in *Varietie of Lute-Lessons* with the title 'The Right Honourable *Ferdinando* Earle of Darby, his Galliard'. The combination of the signs ♯ suggests that a 'fall with a relish' is intended. This would then define the sign ׀ as an appoggiatura from below and the double cross would then probably indicate an appoggiatura from above or a shake according to the length of the note. The single cross + could be a slide — except in one instance, the first chord in bar 10. Here a mordent would be appropriate. Perhaps the sign could be interpreted as meaning either of these two graces.

Lesson 19

No. 50

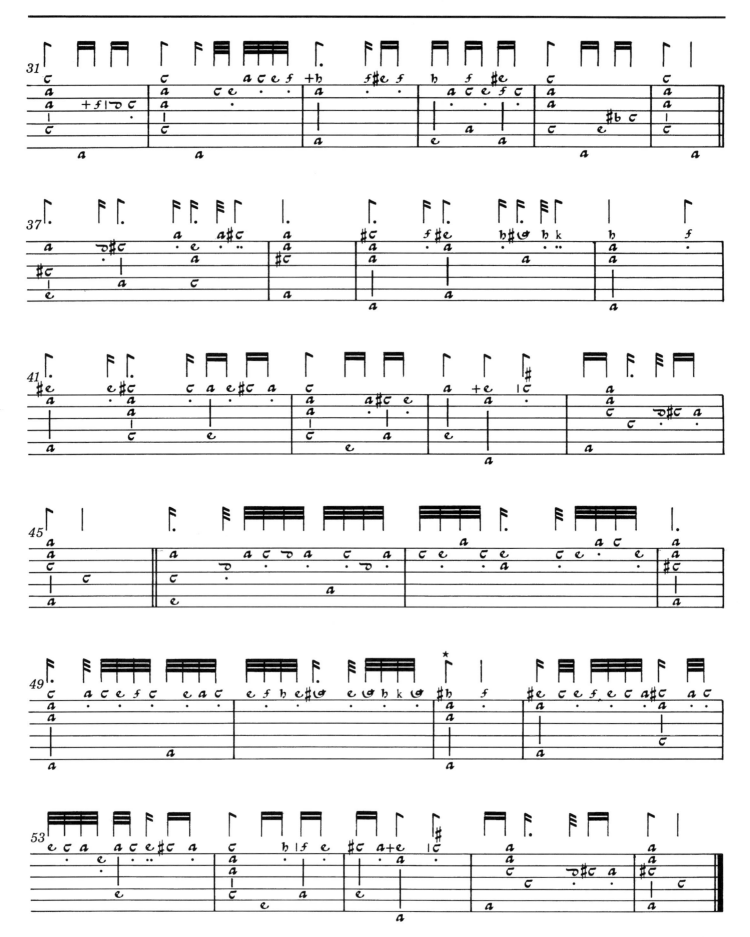

*Time-marks as in MS. They should probably follow the marking of bar 40.

finis a galiard
by m^r Dowland

Lesson 20:
Intabulations of polyphonic vocal music

A large proportion of sixteenth-century lute music consists of intabulations of polyphonic vocal music. In a number of cases the original *chansons*, *madrigali*, *frottole*, etc., have disappeared altogether or only survive with some of the parts missing. A great corpus of this type of music does, however, still exist and, where the songs are available either in the original printed books or in modern editions, it can be helpful, before deciding how the intabulation should be played, to compare it with the original polyphonic version in order to understand the mood of the poem that inspired the music; to obtain a clear idea of how the composer or arranger transferred the vocal lines onto the lute; and to see to what extent diminutions have been added.

The next two pieces come from Pierre Attaingnant, *Tres breve et familiere introduction* (1529) and again show the early form of French tablature. Dotted bar-lines have been added to facilitate comparison with the vocal versions. A translation of the words is given after each *chanson* to convey the mood of the poem. It cannot, of course, in this form be substituted for the original in performance.

No. 51

★ | Appears to equal |.

Il me suffit
Claudin de Sermisy

It is enough of all my sufferings
Since they have handed me over to death,
I have endured pain and travail,
So much grief and misery:
What must I do for you
To stand in your good graces?
With grief my heart is dead
If it look not on your face.

Translation by Alan Robson

No. 51a

Lesson 20

Il me suffit
Claudin de Sermisy

For a note on editorial method see *List of Sources and Modern Editions*.

Another treatment of the polyphonic song which seems to have met with equal approval was in the reduction of the voices to one and the transfer of the others to the lute. The cantus part was the one most generally given to the solo voice but, particularly in Spain, the tenor or even the bassus voice was chosen.

In the case of 'Tant que vivray', the lute solo and the version for solo voice and lute are very close, except for the fact that the last four bars of the lute solo are set out as a repeat for which there is no sign in the version for solo voice and lute.

No. 52

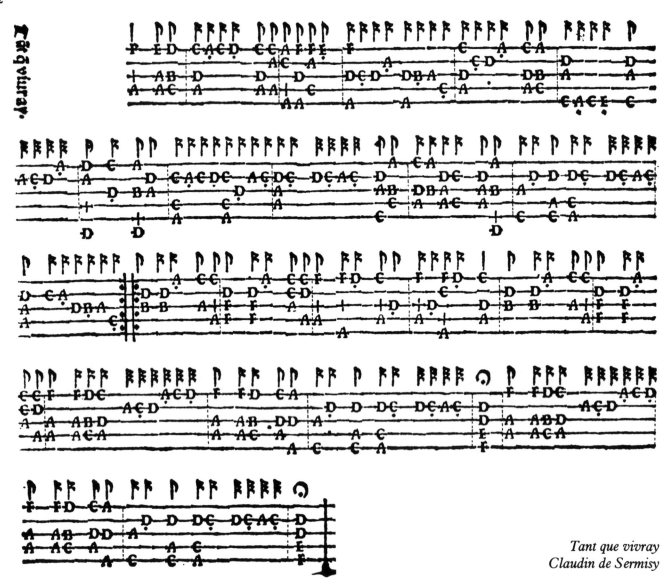

Tant que vivray
Claudin de Sermisy

As long as I shall live in prosperity
I shall serve the powerful god of love
In deeds, in words, in songs and harmony.
For many days I have languished
But after sorrow I am now rejoicing
Because I have the love of the fair lady.
Her union with me is my betrothal,
Her heart is mine and mine is hers,
Fie on sadness! Long live gladness!
For in love there are many blessings.

Translation by Alan Robson

Lesson 20

No. 52a

[T]ant que vi - vray en aa - ge flo - ri - sant
Par plus-ieurs jours m'a te - nu lan - guis - sant
Je ser - vi - ray d'a - mour le dieu puis - sant
Mais a - pres dueil m'a faict re-jou - is - sant
En faictz, en dictz en chan - sons et a - cordz. Son a - li - an - ce
Car j'ay l'a - mour de la bel - le au gent corps.
C'est ma fi - an - ce son cueur est mien Le mien est sien Fi - de tris-tes - se
Vi - ve li - es - se Puis qu'en a-mours Puis qu'en a-mours a tant de biens.

*c on 2 in original in this chord.

No. 53. This very elegant setting for the vihuela of Josquin's 'Mille Regrets' by Luys de Narvaez almost amounts to a composition of his own based on Josquin's theme, since little attempt is made to follow through the contrapuntal voices although the harmonic structure is closely followed. The sadness of the poem is clearly reflected in Josquin's music.

We return here to Italian tablature with the time-marks given exactly as they appear in Narvaez's *Los seys libros del Delphin* (1536).

No. 53

En la quinta en el tercer traste esta la clave de fe fa ut.
En la tercera en el primer traste esta la clave de c sol fa ut.

Lesson 20

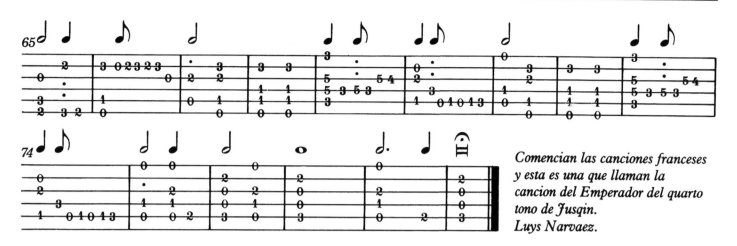

Comencian las canciones franceses y esta es una que llaman la cancion del Emperador del quarto tono de Jusqin.
Luys Narvaez.

A thousand regrets to forsake you
And to leave your loving anger
I have such great grief and doleful pain
That to anyone who sees me
I can only say my days are ended.

Translation by Alan Robson

No. 53a

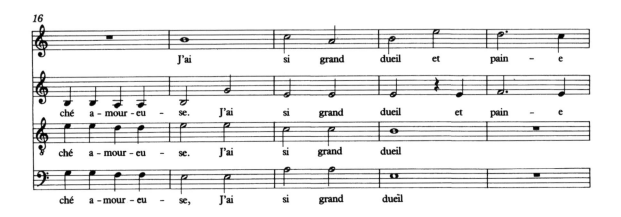

Lesson 21:
The interpretation of signs in the French 'air de cour'

In the accompaniments in many of the books of *airs de cours* which appeared in France from the early years of the seventeenth century onwards, the tablature is heavily marked with signs for right-hand fingering but no explanations are given. Here are some suggestions of what these signs probably mean:

1. All three notes to be played upwards with the first finger alone.
2. All three notes to be played downwards with the back of the first finger.
3. Two notes to be played without the thumb.
4. Three notes to be played without the thumb.
5. and 6. These appear to be a return to the use of the earlier sign to indicate that the notes are to be played without the thumb or they could possibly mean that they are to be played upwards with the first finger alone.
7. This appears to indicate the movement of the bass line.
8. Indicates that the note must be held. Used frequently in the bass.
9. Another hold sign used more frequently for the upper voices.
10. Another sign for indicating the movement of one of the voices, nearly always the bass. It cannot be a sign for *legato* as it sometimes connects notes on different courses.

Nos. 1 and 2 seem to suggest some influence from guitar technique. The downward and upward movement of the first finger is explained by Marin Mersenne in *Harmonie Universelle* (1636).

AIRS

No. 54

Vi prestera la parole A la douleur qui m'affole? Qui donnera les accens A la plainte qui me guide, Et qui lasche-

AIRS

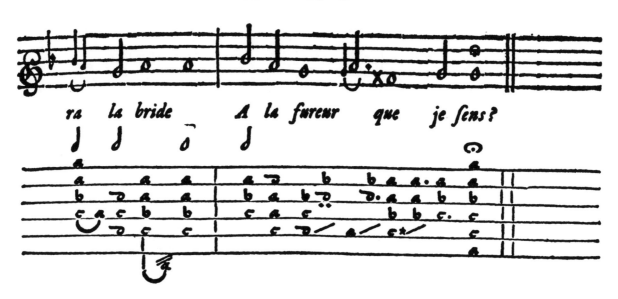

ra la bride A la fureur que je sens?

    Qui baillera double force
A mon ame qui s'efforce
De soupirer ses douleurs?
Et qui fera sur ma face
D'vne larmoyante trace
Couler deux ruisseaux de pleurs?

    Sus mon cœur ouure ta porte,
Afin que de mes yeux sorte
Vne mer à cette fois:
Ores faut que tu te plaignes,
Et qu'en tes larmes tu baignes
Ces montagnes & ces bois.

    Et vous mes vers, dont la course
A de sa premiere sourse
Les sentiers abandonnés,
Fuyés à bride auallée,
Et la prochaine vallée
De vostre bruit estonnés.

    Vostre eau, qui fut claire & lente
Ores trouble & violente,
Semblable à ma douleur soit,
Et plus ne meslés vostre onde
A l'or de l'arene blonde,
Dont vostre fond jaunissoit.

    Mais qui sera la premiere?
Mais qui sera la derniere
De mes plaintes, ô bons dieux!
La furie qui me domte,
Las! je sens qu'elle surmonte
Ma voix, ma langue & mes yeux.

    Vous, à qui ces durs allarmes
Arracheront quelques larmes,
Soyés joyeux en tout temps,
Ayés le ciel fauorable,
Et plus que moy, miserable,
Viués heureux, & contents.

[Didier le Blanc?
Words by Joachim du Bellay]

No. 55

Mounsier Ballard
his Coranto

Lesson 22:
The 'half' barré

The ordinary type of *barré* chord with the first finger of the left hand covering all six courses should already have been mastered completely and it is now time to study some modifications in which the finger does not cover all six courses; for example in the following chord:

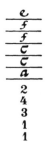

In the next example, in the group of semiquavers in which only four courses are covered, care must be taken to ensure that the tip of the finger does not touch the fourth course and interfere with the clarity of its sound:

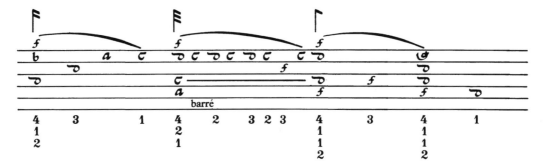

The following examples are also useful for practice:

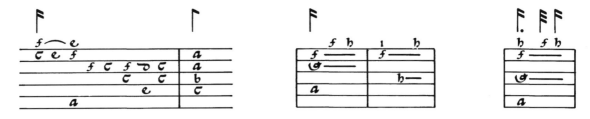

Lesson 23:
German tablature

Many students have a false idea about the problems of reading German tablature but, if Hans Newsidler's system is followed, it will be found far less daunting than is often supposed. There are, however, some difficulties in the very different appearance of the typefaces used, and in the way in which the sixth course and the second alphabet are indicated. We shall, therefore, begin with Newsidler's tablature and then go on to others when the student feels fairly confident in a general understanding of the system.

When originally invented by Conrad Paumann (1410-73) it was designed for a five-course lute. The open courses are numbered 1 to 5 from the fifth course upwards; the frets are then indicated by the letters of the alphabet across the five courses:

Diagram 1

5	e	k	p	v	
4	d	i	o	t	
3	c	h	n	s	z
2	b	g	m	r	y
1	a	f	l	q	x

The letters *u* and *w* are not included. After the first alphabet has been exhausted two frets remain to be filled and these were known as 'et' and 'con'. A great deal of difference is found in the signs used for these frets, as will be seen in some of the facsimile examples of different typefaces shown later.

When notes higher than the fifth fret had to be indicated the alphabet was started again with some distinguishing mark. In Newsidler's books the sign used was a line placed over the letter. Thus the sixth fret on the fifth course would be $\bar{a}$, on the fourth course $\bar{b}$ and so on.

When the sixth course came into general use a method had to be found to identify this and show the frets on it. In Newsidler's case the sixth course is shown by the figure 1 with a line through it: ┼. The capital letters, in a Gothic typeface, continue upwards: A for the first fret, B for the second, C for the third and so on, up to the highest fret on the lute. The following diagram shows this arrangement and also the figures used for *et* and *con*:

Diagram 2

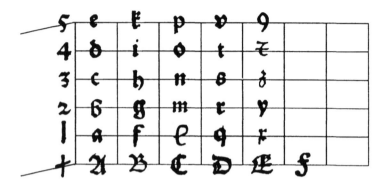

Two of the letters may be puzzling at first: the *k* on the second fret on the top course and, when you come to it, the *x* which is almost indistinguishable from the letter *r* but has a very small tail at the bottom of the left-hand side.

The following is the first of the exercises in Newsidler's books and you should be able to read it if you follow carefully from the diagram. As you will see, there is no stave in German tablature, the letters and figures themselves defining the exact position. The dots over the notes indicate the first finger of the left hand.

No. 56

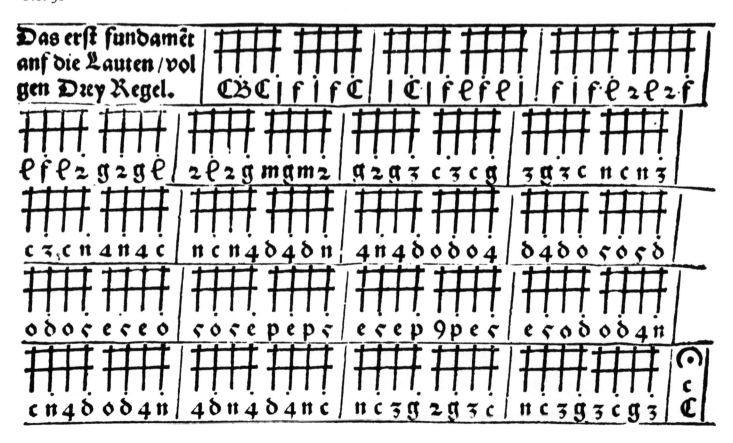

Lesson 23

In the second exercise two notes now have to be played together. The small cross indicates that the note against which it is placed must be held.

No. 57

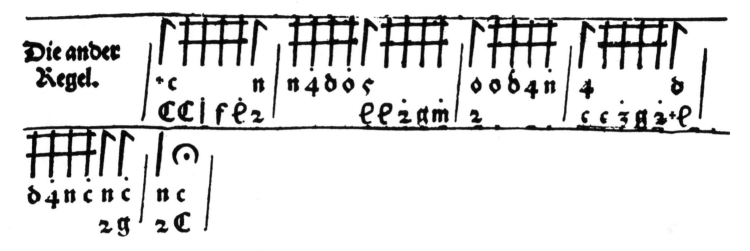

The next six pieces contain only notes that are shown in Diagram 2.

No. 58

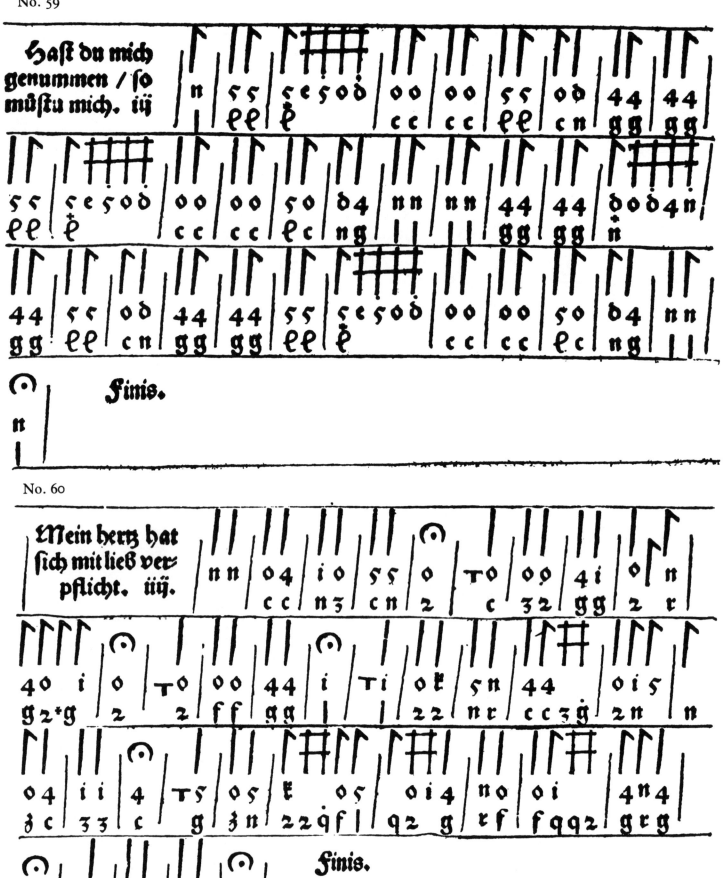

Lesson 23

No. 61

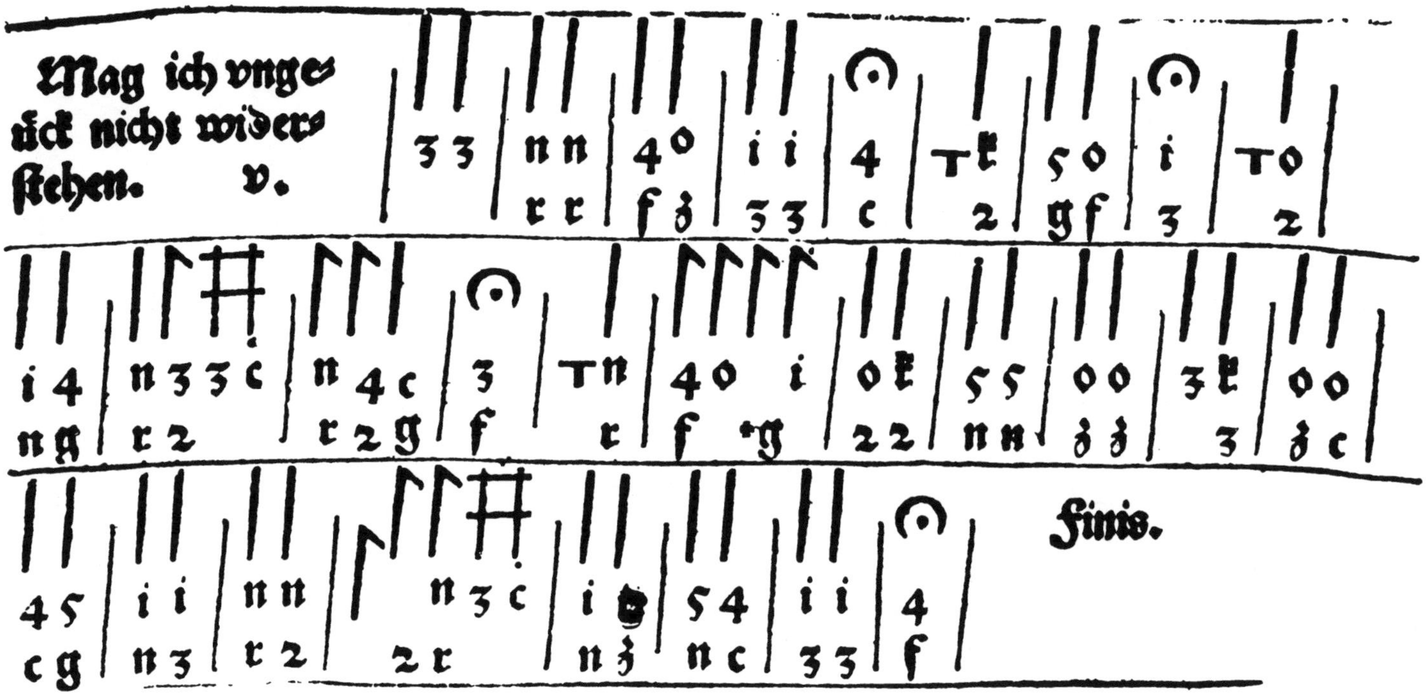

Mag ich vnge=
lück nicht wider=
stehen. v.

finis.

No. 62

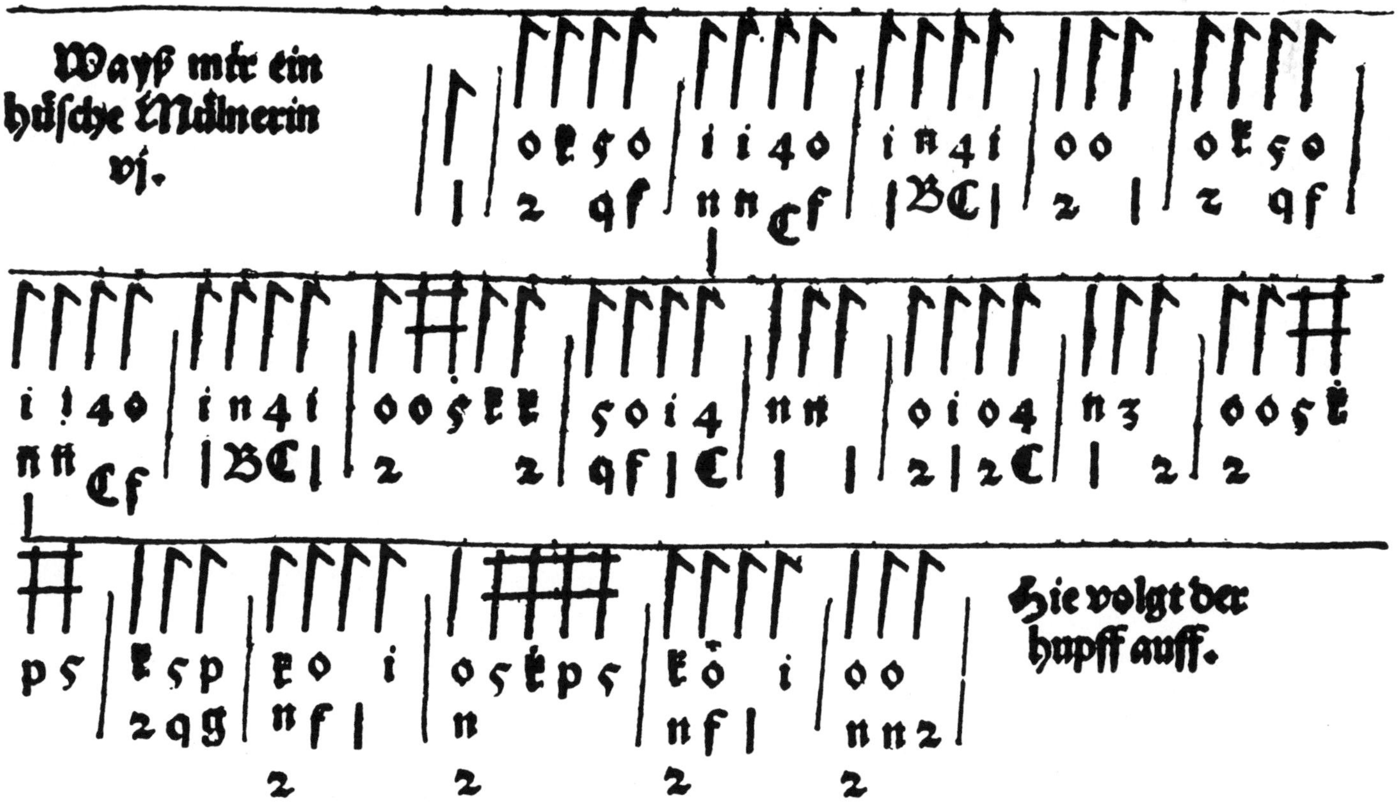

Wayß mir ein
hüsche Mülnerin
vj.

Hie volgt der
hupff auff.

By now the positions of the first alphabet should have been mastered and the *k* of the second alphabet is introduced in bar 10 of 'Der ziegler in der hecken'. This is the equivalent of the letter *h* on 1 in French tablature. In bar 9 of 'Der hupff auff' the lowest of the three signs of the second chord is printed upside down—a fairly common error in German tablature. It is, of course, a 2 as can be seen if the book is turned the other way up. If you are reading a composition and you see a completely unfamiliar sign, turn it up the other way and you may recognize it at once.

Lesson 23

No. 63

Der Ziegler in der hecken. vij.

Der hupff auff.

Finis.

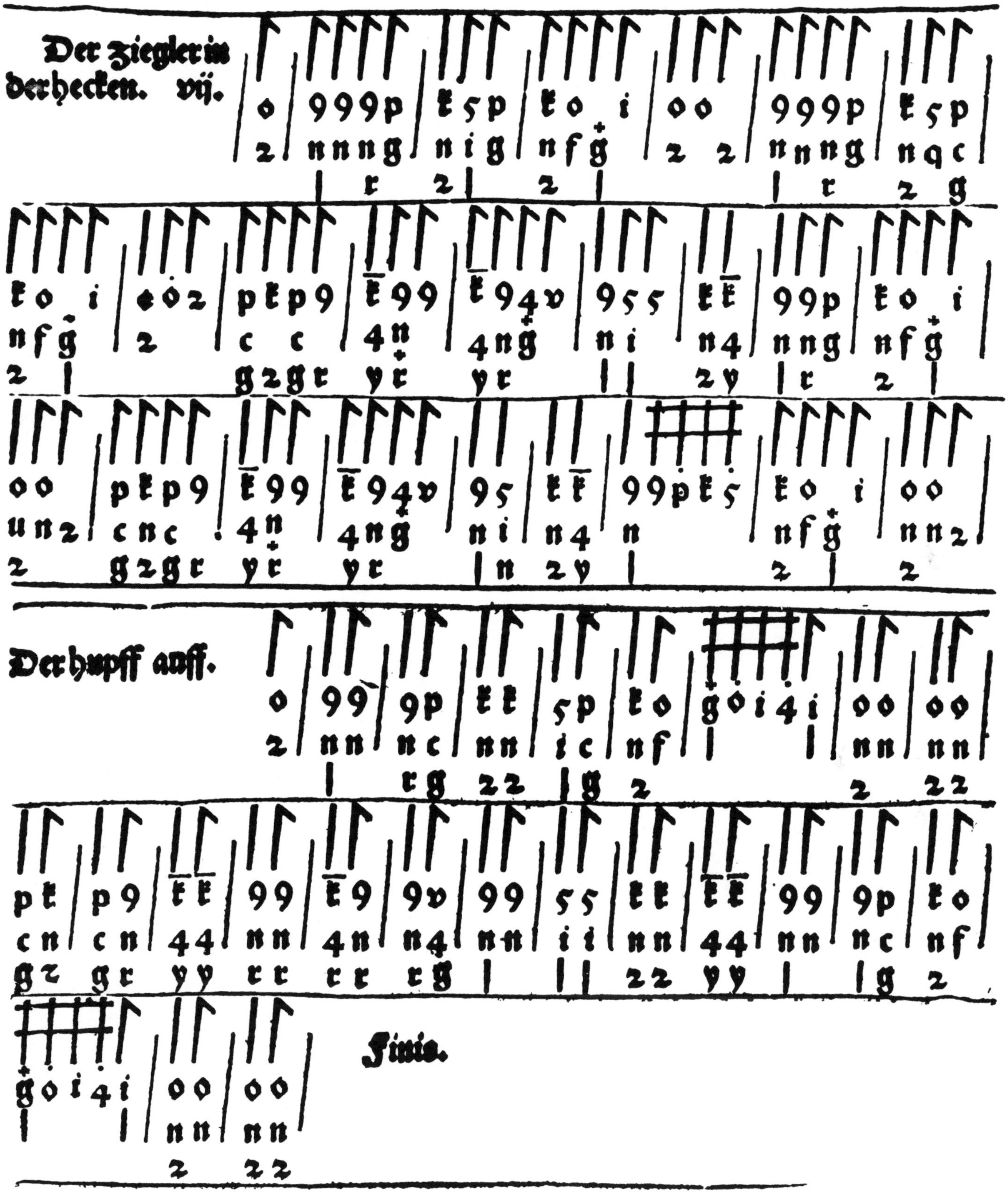

The examples which follow (Nos. 64-9) represent the main typefaces used in German tablature and illustrate most of the signs which may, at first, be difficult to recognize.

No example of the tablature used in Arnolt Schlick's *Tabulaturen Etlicher lobgesang . . .* (Mainz, 1512) is included here since all the signs are easily recognizable. The sixth course is indicated by ┴ and then capital letters beside the same lower-case letters of the fifth course. The accompaniments are all very simple and no second alphabet is used.

No. 64. In Hans Judenkünig's *Utilis & compendiaria introductio . . .* (c. 1519) there is, on sig. Aiii, a diagram of the fingerboard, but the signs shown here are, in some cases, quite different from those used in the text. His system for the sixth course is different from that of Newsidler: his open string is A, the first fret B, the second fret C and so on. In some parts of the book Gothic capitals are used, in others the more usual capitals in use outside the Germanic kingdoms. The right-hand fingering is shown in the time-marks by a little upward tail on the right-hand side ̄F which indicates the first finger. It can be seen that he does not always adhere to the rule that the thumb takes the accented beat. If the first note of a pair lies on a course higher than the second note, the first of the pair will be taken by the first finger and the second by the thumb. When single notes appear they are always printed in the lowest line of letters, irrespective of whether they lie on high or low courses. The sign for the second alphabet is a line above the letter, but it is sometimes smaller and a little less clear than in Newsidler's books.

The following list shows the signs which are more difficult to recognize:

    ꝯ   ('con')

    ⁊   ('et')

    ʒ   (z)

    ſ   (s)   (not to be confused with f)

    ꞇ   (l)

No. 64

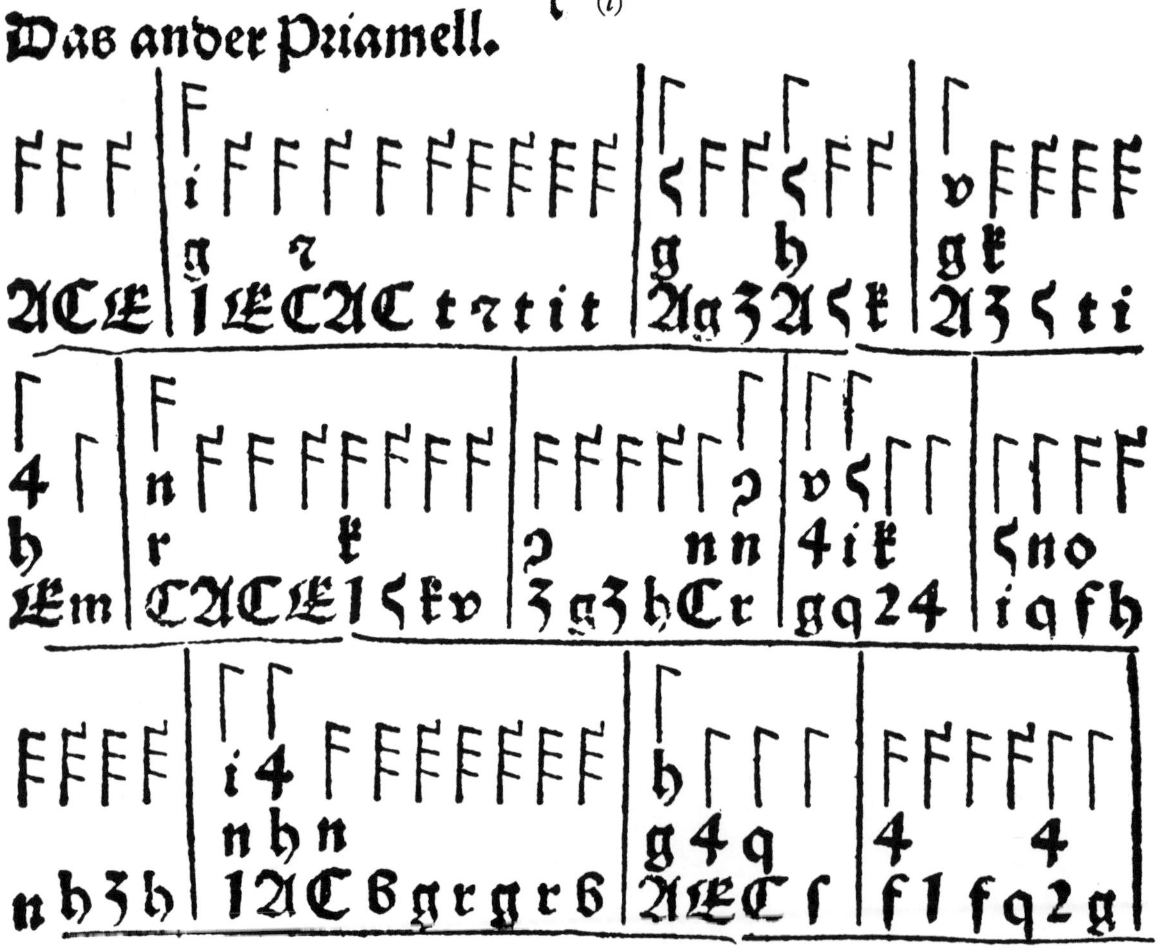

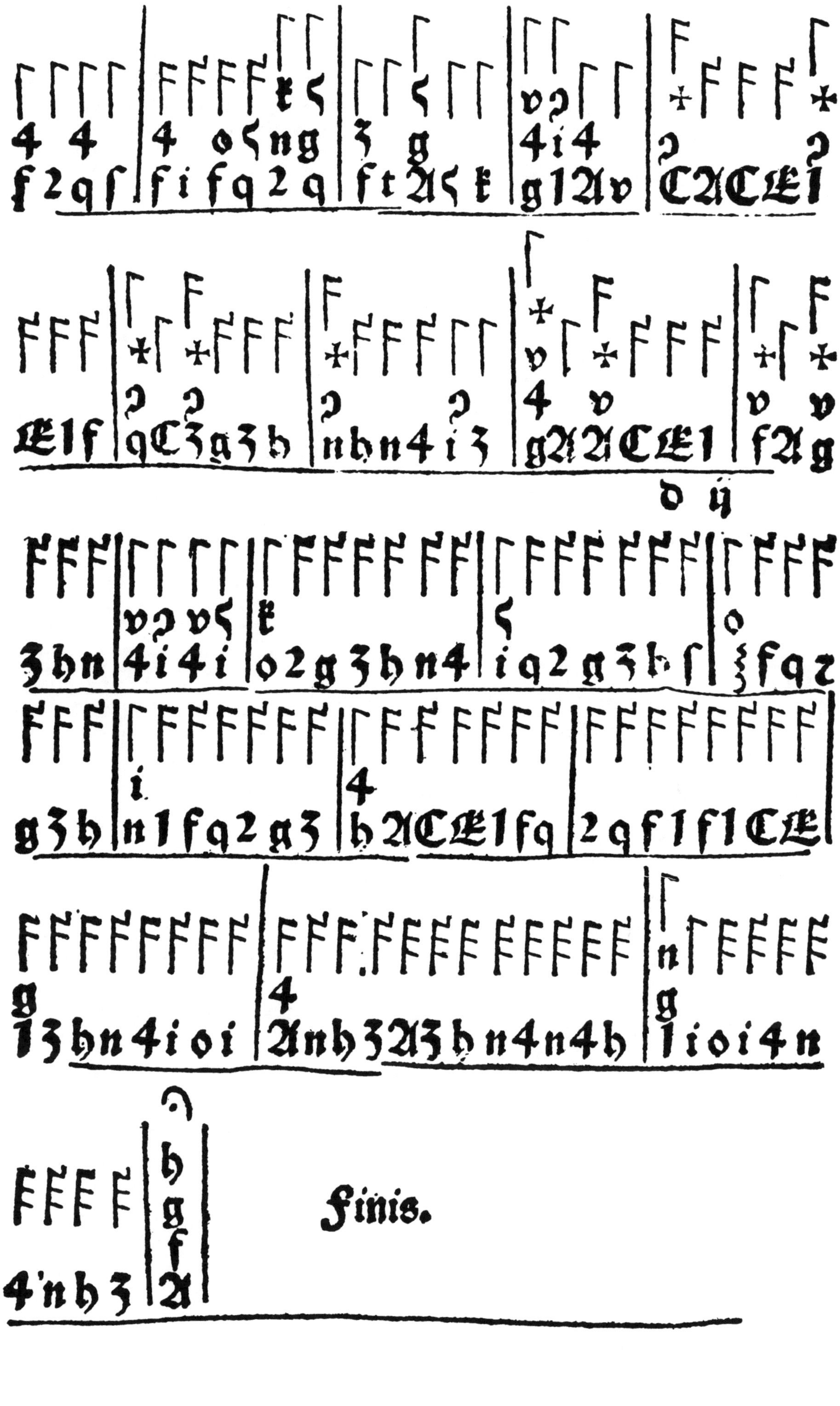
Finis.

No. 65. Hans Gerle's *Musica und Tabulature, auff die Instrument der kleinen und grossen Geygen, auch Lautten . . .* (Nuremberg, 1546) departs from the earlier, heavy typeface and uses an easily legible form. The figure 9 represents the fifth fret on the first course, and the sign under the letter *p* on the third beat of bar 2 represents the fifth fret on the second course. The second alphabet is shown by a curved line over the letters. The sixth course is shown by numbers which proceed upwards with a straight line above each one. In this piece the sixth course has to be tuned a tone lower than its normal pitch, a practice not unusual in Germany and in Italy at this period:

No. 65

Lesson 23

No. 66. The printing in Rudolf Wyssenbach's *Tabulaturbuch uff die Lutten* (Zurich, 1550) is very clear and is far more consistent than that found in many other books, although the sign for the open sixth course is shown sometimes by the figure 1 with a line through, sometimes with a line above. The small figures with a line above for the sixth course continue up the frets until the number five is reached. From then upwards the figures 6, 7, 8, etc., without a line are used. The sign for *et* resembles an upside-down figure 2, ᴢ, and the *con* is rather like a 9 with a little twist in the tail, ℊ. Note the brackets for the appoggiaturas and the small mark on the left-hand side of the signs which shows that the note must be held. (See the List of Sources for information about the contents of this book.)

No. 66

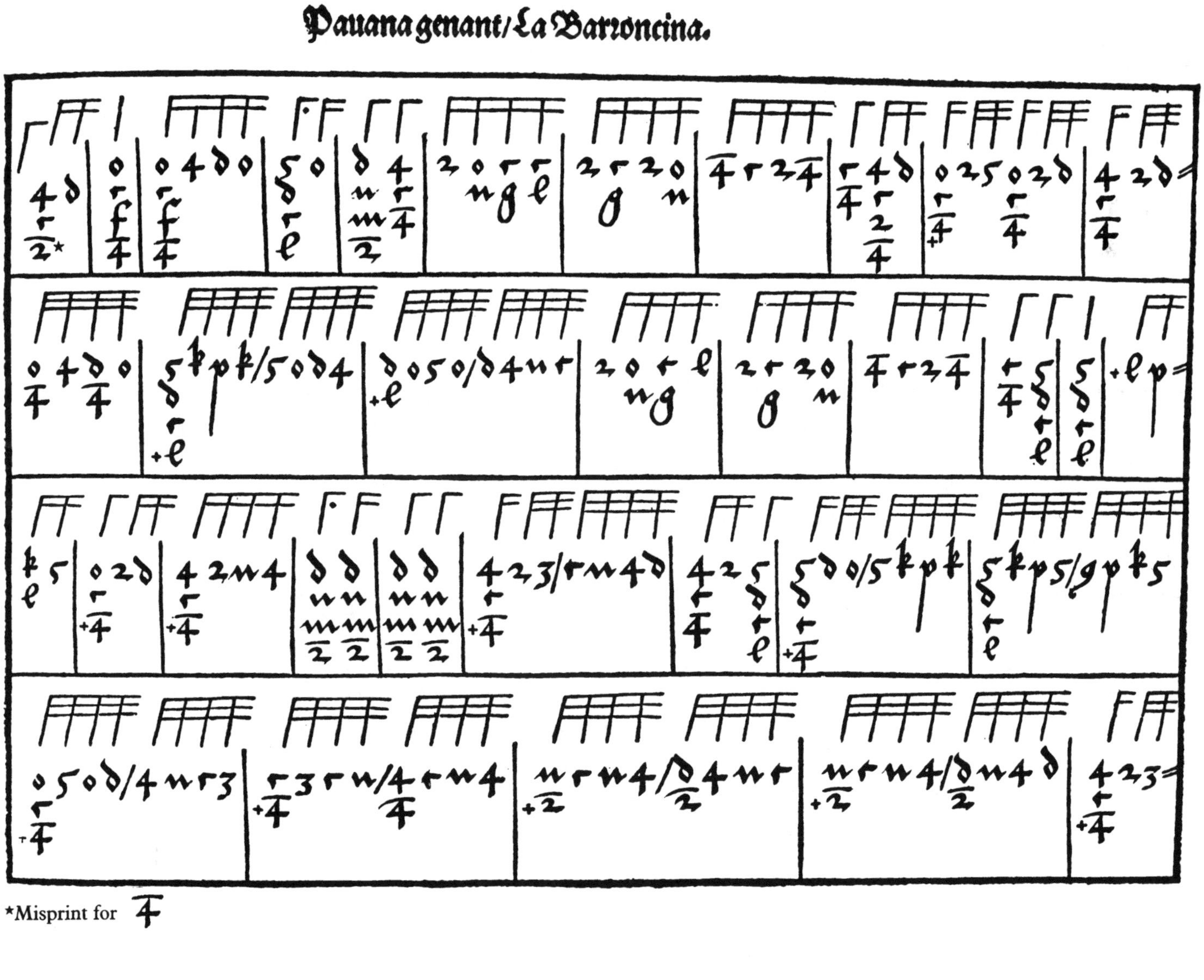

Pauana genant/ La Barroncina.

*Misprint for 𝆑

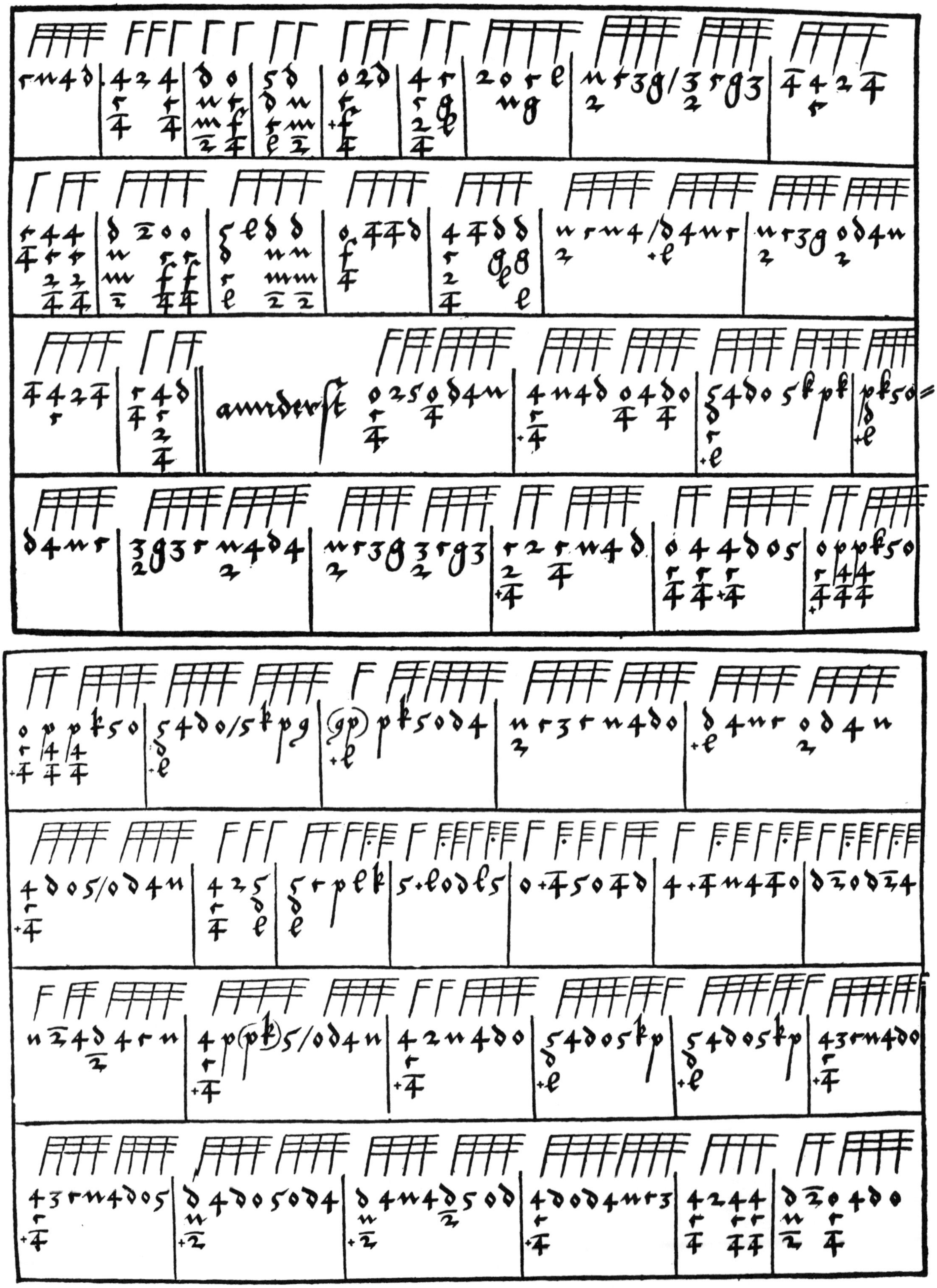

Lesson 23

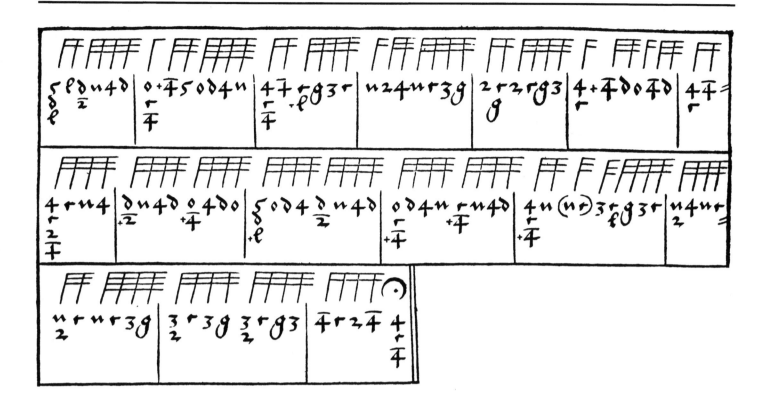

No. 67. This 'Gailliarde' comes from Bernhard Jobin, *Das Ander Buch* (Strasburg, 1573) and illustrates a typeface found in several publications printed in the last quarter of the sixteenth century. The sixth course is indicated by the sign ✱ and then, proceeding up the frets, the same letters are used as those on the fifth course, but with a line through or over each one. Those which lie next to the letters of the second alphabet are shown by double letters (see the last chord in bar 1). A confusing feature of this type of tablature is the fact that the straight and curved line over letters are used indiscriminately for second alphabet and six-course letters.

Here are some of the signs which may, at first, be difficult to recognize:

- ϱ ('con')
- ƶ ('et')
- ꞇ (t)
- ᛵ (i)
- ꞇ (s)
- ᴦ (c)
- ᴦ (r)
- ᶑ (g)
- ᴣ (x)

No. 67

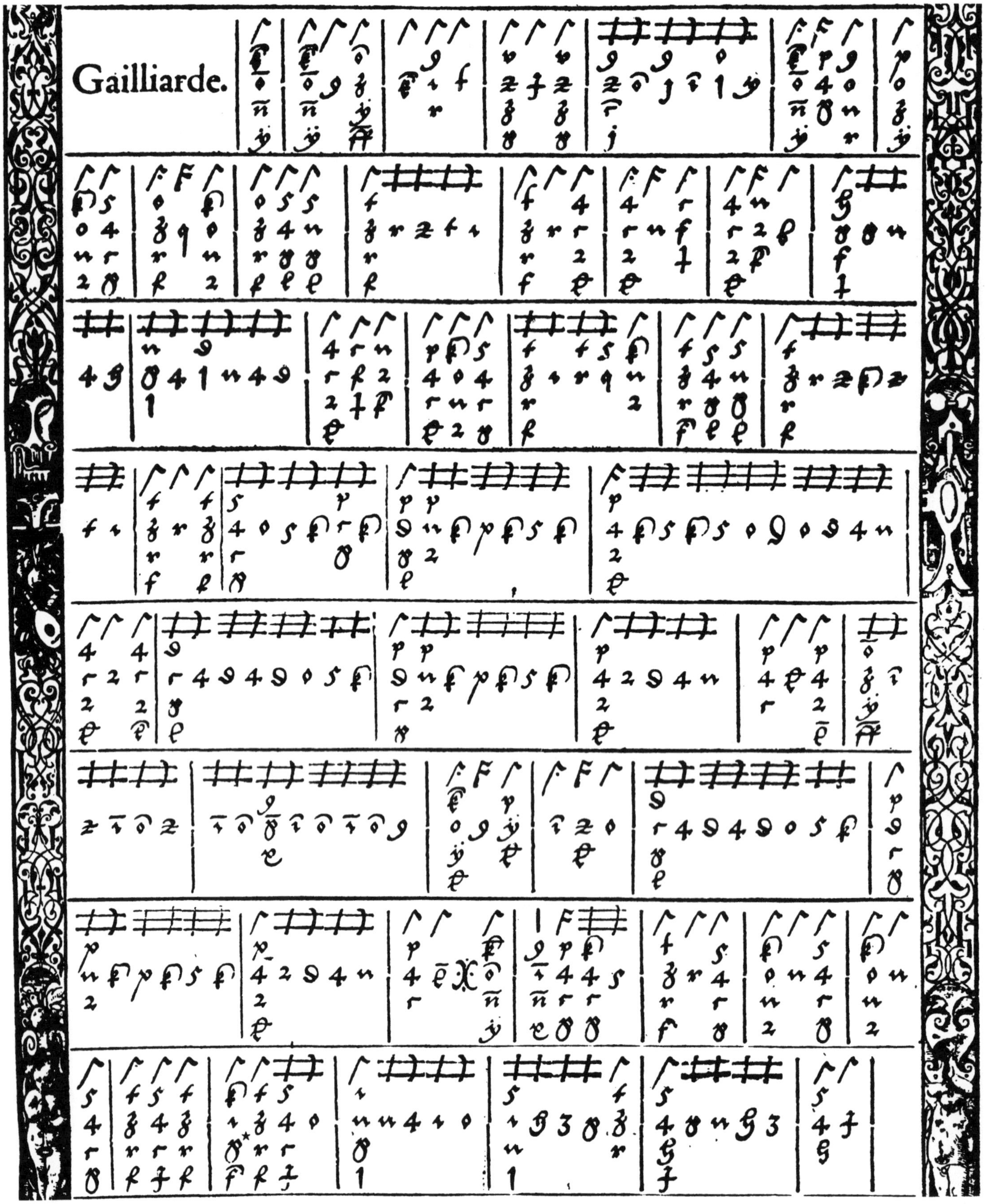

Gailliarde.

*Misprint for the sign 𝑠 (s).

Lesson 23

No. 68. German manuscript tablature can be troublesome because of the idiosyncracies and inconsistencies in the handwriting. The following facsimile comes from 'Lautten Tabulatur' (*c.* 1613) written out by Mikuláš Šmal who was in the employment of Jaroslav Bořita z Martinic (1582-1649), a member of the Czech nobility.

The following diagram shows the form of the signs most generally used. Some of the minor discrepancies are not included.

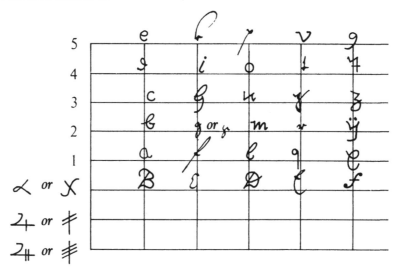

Towards the end of the book the notation of some of the pieces becomes very odd. Chords consist of the letters in their normal position while the numbers are placed in the order of the courses in Italian tablature.

The piece, called 'Englesa', will be recognized as a very poor version of 'Orlando Sleepeth':*

*See *The Collected Lute Music of John Dowland* (London, 1974, 1978, 1981).

Lesson 23

No. 68

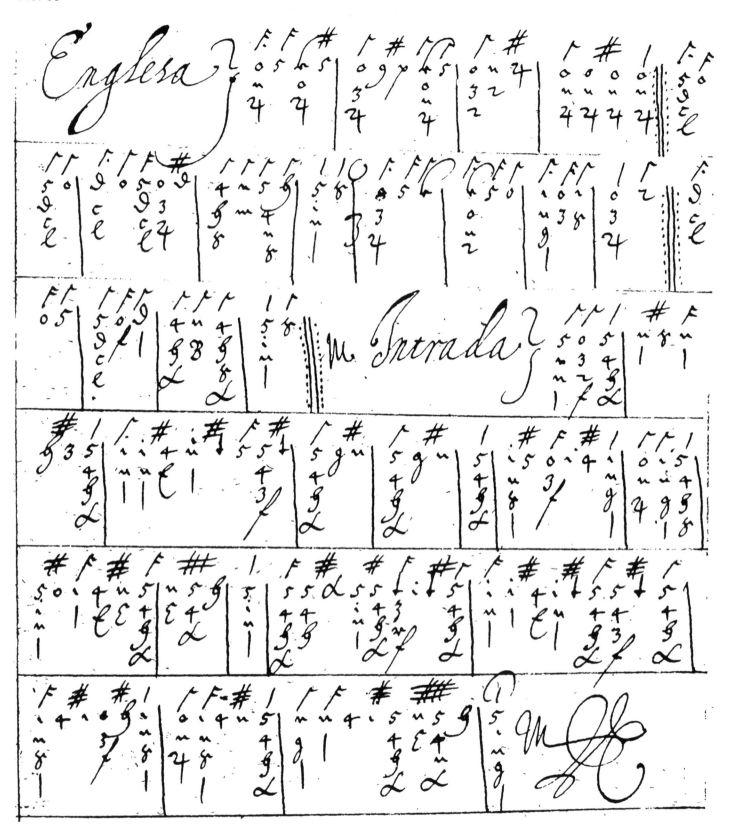

Lesson 23

This Corranto by Laurenzini comes from a large manuscript collection dated 1619. The handwriting is clear and consistent in the shape of the signs used. The open sixth course is shown by a cross and then capital letters proceed upwards. The seventh course is indicated by ‡. The signs in the top line of bar 1 are *k*, *p* and *con*. The only other letter that may be puzzling is *h*, which appears as ʄ :

No. 69

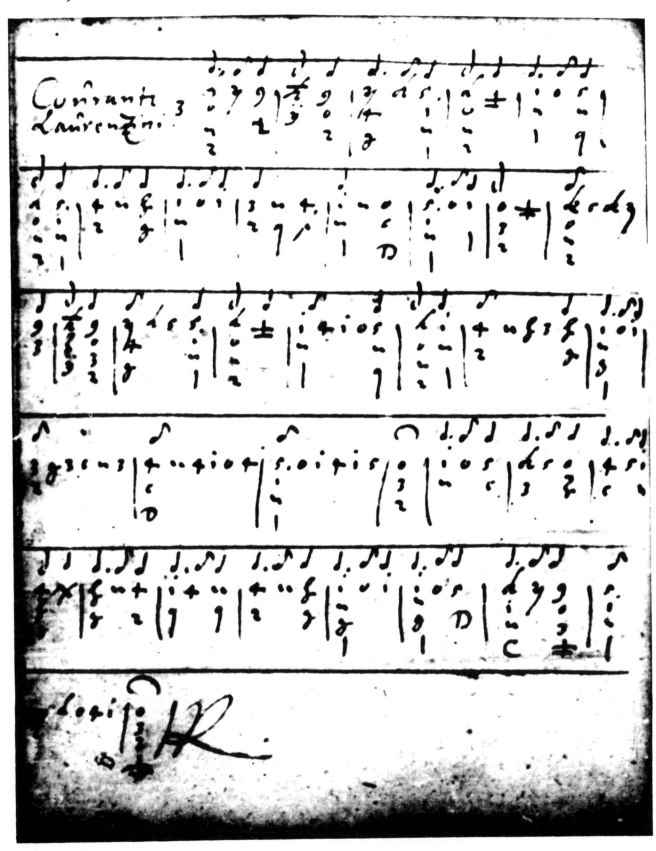

Here, for comparison, is a modern transcription of the manuscript source:

No. 69a

Courante Laurenzini

Lesson 24:
Cifra nueva

Another form of notation in which music for the vihuela is written is the 'new cypher' of Luys Venegas de Henestrosa which appears in his *Libro de Cifra Nueva para tecla, harpa y vihuela* (Alcalá de Henares, 1557). Though primarily a keyboard notation he also recommends it for the vihuela and includes twenty pieces set out for that instrument. His explanations are long and complicated, but they can be summarized as follows: the lines represent each polyphonic voice and range from two to six; the greatest number, including the pieces for the vihuela, being in four parts, the highest line representing the highest voice.

Separate signs are not generally used to show the length of each note or chord, but the position in which the figures are placed within the space of the bar is considered an adequate indication of the note values. Occasionally a dotted note is shown.

The diagram of the keyboard (shown below), although it contains some errors, makes the system clear. The notes from F to e are indicated by the figures 1 to 7. The middle set is shown by plain figures, the lower set by the addition of a small tail (some of these are missing in the diagram), the set below by the tail and a dot (5, 6 and 7 of this set are in the wrong place). Above the middle set the next is shown by a dot after the figure. Two dots indicate a sharp. Where a small 'p' is placed a rest is indicated in that voice until another figure appears on the same line. The flat sign is added where necessary.

The diagram of the vihuela is a curious mixture. The position of the courses is shown as with the highest on the lowest line almost as if it were in Italian tablature, but if the vihuela is placed on its side, as in the diagram, the courses will be the other way up. However, if the six lines are taken as labelled on the right-hand side, the placing of the figure 1 gives F to f' on the first fret with the other figures following in due order giving an E to e' tuning.

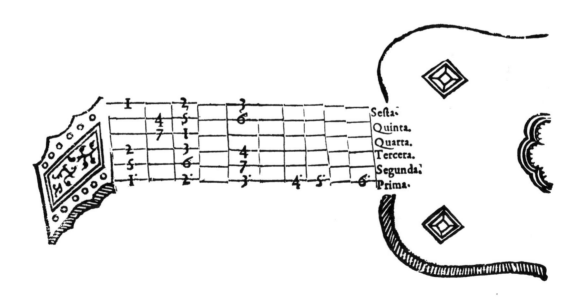

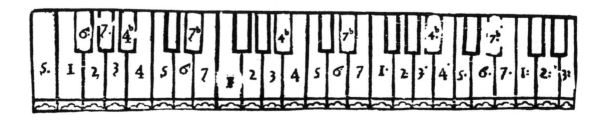

Hernando de Cabeçon uses the same cypher in *Obras de Musica para tecla, arpa y vihuela de Antonio de Cabeçon* (Madrid, 1578). He makes the system clearer by explaining the series of plain figures 1 to 7 in terms of the hexachord: 1 *F fa ut*; 2 *G sol re ut*; 3 *a la mi re*; 4 *b fa* ♮ *mi*; 5 *c sol fa ut*; 6 *d la sol re*; 7 *e la mi*. In staff notation this would read as:

The higher and the lower sets of seven notes are indicated by dots and tails to the figures, as in Venegas de Henestrosa. Flat signs are used where necessary and sharps are shown by a cross placed after the number.

Nos. 70 and 70a.   If the facsimile of this Fantasia from the book by Venegas is compared with the transcription it will be seen how greatly he suffered at the hands of the printer—in this case, the notes of the first three bars and in the placing of the accidentals. Although a long list of *errata* is included at the end of the book, only one from this Fantasia is given. It is interesting to note the curious use of the pause sign in some passages where, it might be expected, the notes should be held. In fact this is impossible as the notes lie on the vihuela in the E to e′ tuning.

No. 70

*The preceding Fantasia ends here.

Lesson 24

No. 70a

*Corrected in the list of errata on fol. xxvi.

Segunda fantesia del quarto tono.
[Anon.]

Lesson 25:
The ten-course lute

The three pieces in this lesson are for a ten-course lute and show the beginning of a change in fashion which was, eventually, to develop into the Baroque style. As has already been seen, lute music in the Renaissance period was closely linked with polyphonic vocal music, while the polyphonic fantasia attracted the attention of many of the greatest composers. Even in dance forms the approach was often much the same, with the polyphonic lines clearly indicated. On the continent, however, change began to show itself among some composers in the early years of the seventeenth century with polyphony giving way to harmonic structure. A far more open texture becomes apparent with *motifs* of an instrumental rather than a vocal character. Although music of this type began to appear in some English collections such as British Library Add. MS 38539, from which No. 71 comes, and some slight evidence of its effect on some younger English composers can be seen, evidence suggests that for a considerable period the works of the great Elizabethan and early Jacobean lutenists continued to dominate the musical scene in England.

In these pieces the student working without a teacher should pay particular attention to the thumb, keeping it in position, not allowing it to jump upwards under the fingers but bringing it to rest on the next course; the only exception to this rule being where a note lies on that particular course which must be avoided with the smallest possible movement. It will be seen, however, in these three pieces how comparatively rarely this happens.

If the student proposes to pass on to the study of Baroque music, the importance of having mastered this particular type of movement with the thumb will become apparent. With a larger number of diapasons it will be found essential to keep the thumb in this contact with the courses, so that a point of reference is maintained and the exact movement of passing one, two, three or whatever the number, either up or down, may be memorized exactly. It will be found to be impossible to do this if the thumb is allowed to fly upwards and the contact is lost. It is an equal impediment to progress if the student allows him- or herself to become dependent on looking at the courses in order to choose the correct one.

In Nos. 71 and 72 the diapasons are tuned at F, E flat and C. In No. 73 the E is natural.

No. 71

*finis
corant*

Courrante du Sieur Mesangeau

Lesson 25

No. 73

Volta
Michaelagnolo Galilei

Lesson 26

Finally, here are two compositions which demand a standard of technical proficiency which would be needed for the final examination in any of the major teaching colleges.

No. 74. The Walsingham ballad appeared in many different versions, generally beginning with the following stanza which appears to be traditional:

> As I went to Walsingham,
>   To the shrine with speed,
> Met I with a jolly palmer
>   In a pilgrim's weed.

The words most usually continue in the form of a sad complaint by a lover who has been deserted by his love. The tune was arranged with sets of divisions by many of the great English composers of the late sixteenth and early seventeenth centuries.

In the chordal passages it is particularly important to obtain the greatest possible continuity of sound by having the left-hand fingering clearly memorized, so that each movement is foreseen and the fingers are ready to make the change without any hesitation.

In the divisions which lie on the upper courses care must be taken to keep the bass notes sounding. When the divisions lie on the lower courses the notes of the melody should be maintained for as long as possible.

No. 74

Lesson 26

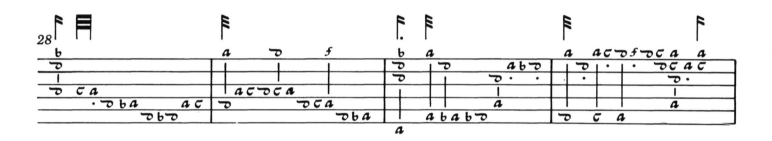

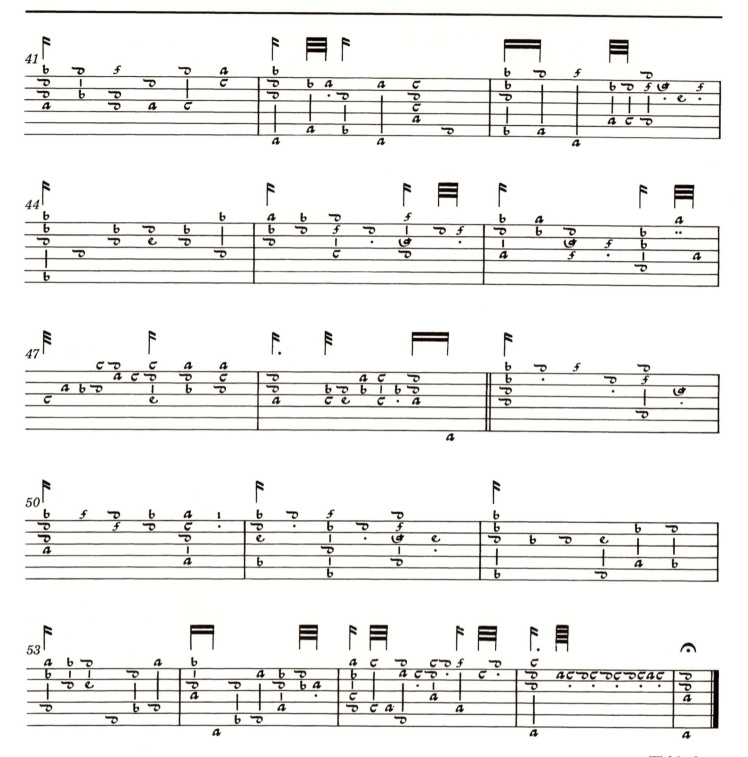

Walsingham
Francis Cutting

Lesson 26

No. 75. This piece is in the conventional form of a pavan, each of the three strains having its decorated repeat. Since the dance was dignified and often performed on stately occasions, the speed at which it should be played is very moderate.

The points mentioned in relation to the preceding piece are of equal importance in the playing of this pavan. The seventh course is tuned at D.

No. 75

Lesson 26

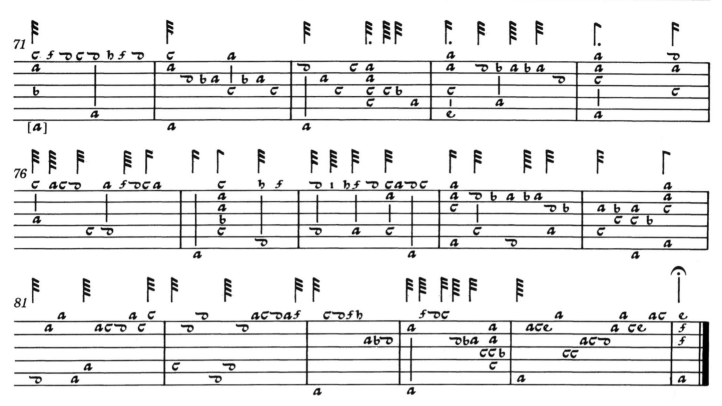

Rosa
John Daniel

List of Sources and Modern Editions

The figure placed beside the date of publication refers to the entry in Howard Mayer Brown, *Instrumental Music Printed before 1600* (Cambridge, Mass., 1967) where lists of contents of each book will be found.

1. Hans Newsidler, *Das Erst Buch* (Nuremberg, 1544$_1$), fol. A4. All the pieces in this book are, of course, in German tablature, but Newsidler was an excellent teacher and arranged a number of pieces specially for beginners.
2. The so-called William Ballet Lute Book, p. 26. See John Ward, 'The Lute Books of Trinity College, Dublin, Ms. D. 1. 21', *The Lute Society Journal* (vol. X, 1968), pp. 15-32.
3. The Jane Pickering Lute Book (1616), fol. 24. British Library MS Eg. 2046. Facsimile edition, Boethius Press (Clarabricken, Ireland, 1985).
4. Ibid. fol. 24.
5. Hans Newsidler, *Das Erst Buch* (Nuremberg, 1544$_1$), fols. 5^v and 6.
6. Ibid. fol. 6.
7. Hans Gerle, *Musica und Tabulatur . . .* (Nuremberg, 1546$_9$), sig. N.
8. Folger Shakespeare Library, Washington, D.C., Music MS 1610. 1., fol. 3.
9. The so-called William Ballet Lute Book, p. 85. See No. 2.
10. Cambridge University Library, Nn. 6. 36, fol. 21, where the name is contracted to 'Pack. Pound.' It is one of the most popular ballad tunes of the seventeenth century.
11. Gordon of Straloch's Lute Book. This MS is now presumed to have been destroyed. 'The Buffens' comes from a selection of pieces copied by G.F.Graham in 1839. National Library of Scotland, Edinburgh, MS Adv. 5. 2. 18.
12. The Jane Pickering Lute Book (1616), fol. 19. British Library MS Eg. 2046.
13. Ibid. fol. 24.
14. Mure of Rowallan's Lute Book, fol. 6. Edinburgh University Library, La. III. 487.
15. Jean-Baptiste Besard, *Thesaurus Harmonicus* (Cologne, 1603), fol. 143^v. Facsimile edition, Minkoff Reprints (Geneva, 1975).
16. Joachim van den Hove, *Delitiæ Musicæ* (Utrecht, 1603), fol. 62.
17. British Library Add. MS 38539, fol. 10. Often erroneously called the John Sturt Lute Book. Facsimile edition, Boethius Press (Clarabricken, Ireland, 1985).
18. Thomas Robinson, *The Schoole of Musicke* (1603), [fol. 29]. Modern edition by C.N.R.S., edited by David Lumsden (Paris, 1971), p. 33.
19. The Schele Lute Book (1619), p. 1. Hamburg Stadtbibliothek, No. ND. VI. 3238. On the flyleaf Ernst Schele wrote 'Musica & vinum lætificant cor hominis'.
20. Ibid. p.1.
21. Ibid. p.1.
22. Jean-Baptiste Besard, *Thesaurus Harmonicus* (Cologne, 1603), fol. 36^v.
23. Pierre Attaingnant, *Tres breve et familiere introduction . . .* (Paris, 1529), fol. ii^v.
24. Albert de Rippe, *Premier Livre de Tabulature de Leut* (Paris, 1552$_8$), fols. 8^v-10^v.
25. Fabritio Caroso, *Il Ballarino* (Venice, 1581$_1$), fol. 39^v.
26. Ibid., fol. 148^v.
27. Antonio Rotta, *Intabolatura de Lauto . . .* (Venice, 1546$_{16}$), fols. 20^v-21.
28. Jiulio Abundante, *Intabolatura di Liuto* (Venice, 1546$_1$), fol. 19.
29. Compositione di meser Vincenzo capirola (*c.* 1517). Modern edition edited by Otto Gombosi (Paris, 1954), p. 83. Facsimile edition, Studio per Edizioni Scelte (Firenze, 1981).
30. Joan Ambrosio Dalza, *Intabulatura de Lauto Libro Quarto* (Venice, 1508$_2$), fol. 16^v.
31. *Intabulatura de Lauto di Francesco Milanese et M. Perino Fiorentino* (Venice, 1547$_2$), sig. A3.
32. Francesco Spinacino, *Intabulatura de Lauto Libro Secondo* (Venice, 1507$_2$).
33. Joan Ambrozio Dalza, *Intabulatura de Lauto Libro Quarto* (Venice, 1508$_2$), fols. 33-34^v.
34. Francesco Milanese (Francesco da Milano), *Intavolatura de viola o vero lauto* (Naples, 1536), Libro Secondo, fols. 30^v-31. (Not listed in Brown.) Facsimile edition, Minkoff Reprint (Geneva, 1977). Libro Primo is in ordinary Italian tablature, Libro Secondo is in

List of sources and modern editions

Intavolatura alla Napolitana, but there is a serious error in the binding of the original edition: from folio 29 onwards the folios from Libro Primo and Libro Secondo have been interchanged. This fault has not been corrected in the facsimile.

35. Luys Milan, *El Maestro* (Valencia, 1536₅), sig. B1ᵛ. Modern edition edited by Leo Schrade (Leipzig, 1927, reprinted Hildesheim, 1967), p. 2.
36. Ibid., sig. D2ᵛ. Modern edition, p. 54.
37. Ibid., sig. D6. Modern edition, p. 60.
38. Alonso Mudarra, *Tres Libros de Musica en Cifras para Vihuela* (Seville, 1546₁₄), fol. 1.
39. Luys de Narvaez, *Los seys libros del Delphin* (Valladolid, 1538₁), Il sesto libro, fols. lxxxii-lxxxvi.
40. Miguel de Fuenllana, *Orphenica Lyra* (Seville, 1554₃), fol. clixᵛ.
41. *Compositione di meser Vincenzo capirola*. See No. 29 above, modern edition, p. 83, facsimile, p. 96.
42. *Intavolatura di Lauto del Divino Francesco da Milano, et dell'Eccellente Pietro Paulo Borrono* (Milan, 1548₃), fol. 11ᵛ.
43. Nicolas Vallet, *Paradisus Musicus Testudinis* (Amsterdam, 1618), p. 52.
44. Nicolas Vallet, *Piété Royale* (Amsterdam, 1620), p. 113.
45. William Barley, *A new Booke of Tabliture* (London, 1596₄), sig. Dᵛ.
46. The Weld Lute Book (c. 1600), fol. 8. In the possession of Lord Forester. See Robert Spencer, 'The Weld Lute Manuscript', *The Lute Society Journal* (vol. I, 1959), pp. 48-57.
47. Folger Shakespeare Library, Washington, D.C., Music MS 1610. 1., fols. 10ᵛ-11.
47a. British Library, London, Add. MS 38539, fols. 12ᵛ-13. (See No. 17.)
48. Ibid. fols. 14ᵛ-15.
49. Ibid. fol. 16.
50. The Sampson Lute Book, fol. 13ᵛ. In the possession of Robert Spencer, Woodford Green, Essex. Facsimile edition, Boethius Press (Clarabricken, Ireland). Introduction and concordances by Robert Spencer.
51. Pierre Attaingnant, *Tres breve et familiere introduction* . . . (Paris, 1529₃), fol. xxxixᵛ.
51a. Claudin de Sermisy, *Twenty Chansons*, No. 10. Modern edition by London Pro Musica Edition, edited by Bernard Thomas. The note values have been halved; the accidentals taken from keyboard or lute intabulations are printed on the stave in brackets and apply to the whole bar. Purely editorial accidentals appear above the stave and apply to one note only.
52. Pierre Attaingnant, *Tres breve et familiere introduction* . . . (Paris, 1529₃), fol. liiiᵛ.
52a. Ibid., fol. livᵛ.
53. Luys de Narvaez, *Los seys libros del Delphin* (Valladolid, 1538₁), fols. lxxxii-lxxxvi.
53a. Modern edition, see *Josquin des Prés: Werken*, ed. Albert Smijers, 1921—.
54. Gabriel Bataille, *Livre d'Airs de differents autheurs mis en tablature de luth par Gabriel Bataille* (Paris, Pierre Ballard, 1613), fol. 57ᵛ. The words are by Joachim du Bellay, the music probably arranged by Bataille from the four-part setting by Didier Le Blanc, of which the contratenor part is now lost. The *air* is included in *Airs de Cour pour Voix et Luth* (1603-1643). *Transcription avec une introduction et des commentaires par André Verchaly* (Paris, 1961), p. 46.
55. Robert Dowland, *Varietie of Lute-Lessons* (London, 1610), sig. Qᵛ. Facsimile edition by Schott and Co. Ltd (London, 1958), p. 62.
56. Hans Newsidler, *Ein newes Lautenbuchlein* (Nuremberg, 1540₁), 'Das erst fundament auf die Lauten volgen Drey Regel', sig. Aiiᵛ. In this book the binding signatures at the bottom of the pages are very confused, so, except for the first and the second exercise, the numbering of the pieces follows that of Newsidler.
57. Ibid., 'Die ander Regel', sig. Biii.
58. Ibid., No. ii.
59. Ibid., No. iii.
60. Ibid., No. iiii.
61. Ibid., No. v.
62. Ibid., No. vi.
63. Ibid., No. vii.

64. Hans Judenkünig, *Ain schone kunstliche underweisung in disem büchlein* . . . (Vienna, 1523$_2$), sig. dii-dii^v.
65. Hans Gerle, *Musica und Tabulatur auff die Instrument der kleinen und grossen Geygen, auch Lautten* (Nuremberg, 1546$_9$), sig. Zii^v-Ziii^v.
66. Rudolf Wyssenbach (publisher), *Tabulaturbuch uff die Lutten* . . . (Zurich, 1550$_4$). The compositions in this book are all transcriptions into German tablature from *Intabulatura di Lauto del Divino Francesco da Milano et dell'Eccellente Pietro Paulo Borrono* (Venice, 1546$_8$), fols. 4-5^v.
67. Bernhardt Jobin, *Das Ander Buch* (Strasburg, 1573$_2$), sig. D4-D4^v.
68. Mikuláš Šmal z Levendorfu MS (*c*. 1615), Prague University Library, MS XXIII F 174. Facsimile edition, Sumptibus Pragopress (Prague, 1969).
69. Leipzig, Musikbibliothek der Stadt Leipzig, MS II 6. 15., p. 256.
70. Luys Venegas de Henestrosa, *Libro de Cifra Nueva Para Tecla, Harpa, Y Vihuela* (Alcalá de Henares, 1557$_2$). From the group of pieces listed in the Table of Contents, under the heading 'Tiento de los ocho tonos, de vihuela', fol. xxxvii.
71. British Library, Add. MS 38539, fol. 26^v. (See No. 17.)
72. Ioannes Baptista Bersardus, *Novus Partus* (Augsburg, 1617), p. 43.
73. Michaelagnolo Galilei, *Il Primo Libro d'Intavolatura di Liuto* (Munich, 1620), p. 12.
74. William Barley, *A new Book of Tabliture for the Orpharion* (London, [1596]) sig. D2-3
75. Cambridge University Library, Add. MS 3056, fols. 18^v-19.